War on Jihadism By Ideology:
The New Islamic Religious Revolution

Dr. Yassin El-Ayouty, Esq.

DR. YASSIN EL-AYOUTY, ESQ.

ISBN: 1979932182
ISBN-13: 978-1979932189

DEDICATION

To Al-Azhar Al-Sharif and to its Grand Imam, Dr. Ahmed El-Taiyeb, in recognition of the launching of the New Islamic Religious Revolution through Azhari thought and teaching. Countering the chaos generated world-wide by jihadism.

My spiritual link to Al-Azhar began with my early education at the hands of my late Azhari father, Sheikh El-Sayed Muhammad Hassanain El-Ayouty.

The thoughtful interpretation of Islam as a continuum with all other faiths, presented by the Grand Imam of Al-Azhar in speeches in Germany, Nigeria, France, Russia, the United Arab Emirates, and Egypt, has been the primary inspiration of this book. It is therefore only fitting to also annex to this volume a biographical note on Dr. Ahmed Muhammad El-Taiyeb.

DR. YASSIN EL-AYOUTY, ESQ.

TABLE OF CONTENTS

DR. YASSIN EL-AYOUTY, ESQ.

FOREWORD

The themes of this book have been in my head since Islamophobia in the West, especially with the rise of the ultra-right, degenerated into anti-Islamism. Jihadism which has been waging terrorism globally under the guise of Islam contributed greatly to lending that anti-Islamism a raison d'etre.

With the two negative currents converging and becoming mutually self-justifying, Islam as a faith, and global security as a cherished value became the objects of skepticism. An enhancer of these trends has been the absence of translation of Arabic into other main languages. An example of this is the efforts by Al-Azhar Al-Sharif and its Grand Imam, Dr. Ahmed El-Taiyeb, exerted primarily from Cairo, are not well publicized in non-Arabic speaking areas. In that vacuum, both jihadism and anti-Islamism, crept in, nearly unchallenged.

It took nearly a year to produce this volume as a modest contribution to the war on jihadism by ideology -the least used weapon in this war. The pace of authorship has been slowed by the need to translate and document. Repetition of the same evidence from scripture has been unavoidable due to the overlapping nature of the issues raised.

I consider it an honor to dedicate this book to Al-Azhar, in support of its New Islamic Religious Revolution which the leadership of the New Egypt, both secular and religious, have called for. And to the many individuals who have assisted me all along in this complex task, the acknowledgments do not suffice in reflecting my deep gratitude to all and everyone of them.

In the rush to have this book published, I have no doubt that I perhaps should have done more in adhering to the strictures of writing a book covering faith, law, politics, attitudes, and style. It is my hope that the reader would be forgiving of my shortcomings which I would be the first to concede their occurrence. However, the psychic pleasure of joining through this book the struggle against jihadism, wrongly phrased as Islamic terrorism, has its way of offering me a subdued sense of satisfaction.

Nothing could better sum up the thesis of this book like a heartfelt lament by an Egyptian Coptic clerk in the wake of a jihadi attack on a church in Sinai in October 2017. Following that coward criminality at El-Arish, Sinai, Egypt, the spokesman for the Coptic church, Bishop Boulos

Halim, said: **"Terrorism shall persist until we drain its swamps. To do this, we must create an enlightened environment capable of dissipating this obscurantist thought. This is the way to re-establish sound human relationships, to enhance and nurture values and creativity. Security measures, standing alone in the face of terrorism, do not suffice."**

Some intellectuals, like Dr. Hesham Elnakib, object to the term **"Jihadism."** Their concern is well taken as that term might cast aspirations on **"Jihad"** in its proper Islamic context. Though this volume contains a chapter entitled **"Jihad and Criminality Don't Mix,"** yet Elnakib's reservation has the merit of stressing that our use of **"Jihadism"** is intended to be equated with **"terrorism in the name of God."**

ACKNOWLEDGMENTS

It is with humility that I acknowledge those whose assistance was crucial in having this work see the light of day. Following my wife Grace El-Ayouty, and son Joseph El-Ayouty are, in various capacities and in alphabetical order are:

Mr. Tarek Allagany
Mr. Raymond Chan
Dr. Hala Hassan El-Ayouty
Vittoria Fariello, Esq.
Dr. Kamal Abdel-Salam Hassan
Ms. Alison Izzo
Carolina Maluje, Esq.
Rossalyn Quaye, Esq.
Mr. Wagdy Rizk
Dr. Zahra Hend Shnayen
Mr. Ahmed Yousri

Their help, in various ways, particularly that of our Webmaster, Mr. Raymond Chan, has been invaluable. Any errors or critical omissions are entirely my own responsibility.

DR. YASSIN EL-AYOUTY, ESQ.

CHAPTER 1

Introduction

The objective of the New Islamic Religious Revolution is to delegitimize jihadism. Jihadism is the conversion of Islam as a faith into a combatant against Muslims and non-Muslims alike. ISIS, Al-Qaeda, Al-Nusra Front, Boko Haram and Al-Shabab are all jihadi organizations using terrorism as a weapon for intimidation, power and illegitimate control. All in the name of the faith of 1.7 Billion Muslims who, together with all other adherents of any faith have, since 1998, paid a heavy price exacted by jihadism.

The use of the term **"jihadism"** has two purposes: avoiding the misnomer of **"Islamic terrorism,"** as no form or tool of terrorism should be associated with any faith. And to provide a chance for explaining in this introduction what the real and correct meaning of Jihad is all about.

"Jihad," in Arabic, means striving or exertion. In Islamic jurisprudence **"Sharia,"** jihad has two meanings: the inner struggle within any human being against one's base urgings -self-policing. And self-defense against internal or external aggression against sovereign territory, its people, its resources, and its security.

This latter form of jihad is governed by strict rules. First among them is its containment within the national boundary. The second is the readiness to negotiate with that adversary for the final resolution of the situation which motivated that aggression. In Islam, there is no **"holy war"** -a term generated by western thought. As a matter of fact, there is not even one mention in the Quran of the word **"saif"** **(sword).**

The torch bearer of this New Islamic Religious Revolution is Al-Azhar, the citadel in Cairo established nearly 1050 years ago as the seat for moderate and inclusive Islamic learning. Now headed by a great thinker, a graduate of the Sorbonne in Paris, its Grand Imam, Dr. Ahmed El-Taiyeb.

As two successive revolutions erupted in Egypt (January 2011 and June 2013), the post-Islamist president of Egypt, Abdel-Fattah El-Sisi, called on that citadel of Islamic scholarship to accelerate its New Islamic Religious Revolution as a weapon against terrorism in Sinai, on the borders of Libya, and within the country itself.

It had become clear in Egypt and beyond that the sacking of Islamist Brotherhood rule in the country of 7000 years would generate a hostile and bloody response by the collapsed Brotherhood. The battle lines were sharply drawn as of July 3, 2013 between a rejected so-called Islamic rule, and a secular rule which is a part of Egypt's DNA since the days of the pharaohs.

In response, the voice of Al-Azhar, which as of 2015 I was invited to represent in America and Canada as its Focal Point, was uttered by the Grand Imam Ahmad El-Taiyeb from August 2011 to the end of 2016. This is the span of time which this book shall deal with.

Its material is primarily based on the conceptualization of the various statements made in Arabic by the Grand Imam in various international locations in Europe and the Middle East. And secondarily by my own work, drawn from nearly weekly blog postings as they dealt with **"Islamism vs. Secularism,"** and from my teaching and other writings on the same issue. Other outside sources have been pressed in the service of this novel introduction of the New Islamic Religious Revolution.

Presenting this ideology at a time in America and the rest of the world, when the voice of ISIS and its kin jihadi franchises has overwhelmed the precepts of Islam, is a professional duty on my part. I regard it as a contribution to the security of America and other affected parts of the world. For it must be recognized that there is a strong and undeniable linkage between Islamic Law (fiqh) or (Sharia) and global security.

Yet regardless of the timeliness, the cogency, and the veracity of the New Islamic Religious Revolution, its success shall also depend on auxiliaries. The most important of such auxiliaries are American leaders inside as well as outside the White House now occupied by an anti-Islamist, Donald J. Trump. They have the primary obligation in assisting in the defense of America through their abstaining from attacking Islam and Muslim

Americans, in consequence of their adoption of attitudes based on the ideology of jihadism.

It should be here noted that nothing contained in this book is intended as whitewashing the malevolent practices of anti-jihadis, principal among them are the Wahhabis. Though begun in the 19th Century as a reform movement in Arabia by Muhammad Ibn Abdel-Wahhab, Wahhabism degenerated into a retrograde theocracy which placed a premium on the literal and obscurantist interpretation of the Quran, and the Hadith (the Sunna of the Prophet Muhammad).

Its mischief, made formal by its concordat with the Second Saudi State under its founder King Abdel-Aziz Ibn Saud. Chief among the elements of that sharing of power has been the treatment of women, its emphasis on the role of the religious police, and its intolerance towards its Shii population. All too lamentable.

There is a reason why 15 of the 19 criminals who attacked America on 9/11 were Saudis. That was not an accident. It was the result of the poisonous fruit emerging from poisonous roots. Ironically, the Kingdom of Saudi Arabia itself has also been the victim of its continuing to give free reign to the Wahhabis -the co-rulers in the realm of faith.

It is hoped that the New Islamic Religious Revolution, as launched by Al-Azhar under its inspired Grand Imam, Sheikh Ahmed El-Taiyeb, would help in containing the global consequences not only of jihadism, but also of the negative advocacy of a mythical Islam advanced by misguided thought in the America of Trump, in Saudi Arabia of the Wahhabis, and in the madrasas in South East Asia. These madrasas have been funded by petrodollars and enhanced by calling **"the other"** as an infidel.

Authoring this volume as of January 2017, it is to be hoped that by the time it is on the bookshelves later this year, the war against ISIS and its confederates wherever they may be, would have made my conclusions a bit obsolete. It is this kind of obsoleteness which can only be read as progress towards an inter-faith world. Such world is the heart of this new revolution.

This is a book delineating fact from fiction. Its primary inspiration and documentation have been drawn heavily from the statements made on the world stage by the Grand Imam of Al-Azhar, Dr. Ahmed El-Taiyeb. To him, and to the culture of warring on jihadism, this book owes its very existence to the Al-Azhar culture.

What makes of the New Religious Revolution a weapon of mass destruction in the war on jihadism is its provision of specific responses. These responses are anchored in the Quran and the Sunna of the Prophet Muhammad. To these anchors, we should also add ijtihad (the use of reason to interpret issues on which no such texts exist to dispose of it.)

The issues which are forcefully addressed as a coherent ideology of the New Islamic Religious Revolution, whose banner is raised aloft by the Grand Imam of Al-Azhar, include the following:
1. Countering jihadi concepts. Important among them is that Islam is not a unique faith with a monopoly on wisdom, denying the sanctity and role of other faiths;
2. While jihadism practices killing and destruction, the New Islamic Religious Revolution (NIRR) confronts this nihilism as besmirching Islam. NIRR posits the idiocy of that jihadi nihilism as the latter espouses the viewpoint that traditional values and beliefs are unfounded;
3. Islam is not the preserve of only those who are born Muslims. It is a title in which all of humanity shares as individuals, regardless of any faith they espouse. Its kernel is the submission by the individual of his/her will to that of the Creator;
4. There is plenty of guidance and light in both the Torah and the New Testament;
5. Belief in humanity as an entity is the gateway to other non-revealed faiths, such as Buddhism and Confucianism. Such belief constitutes an integral part of the tapestry of faith in the invisible; and
6. Religions should not be judged by the acts of the criminal few. What arches over beliefs, or even non-belief, is **"the law of diversity."**

The central issue with which this book deals is the developing ideological confrontation, mainly by Al-Azhar, against jihadism. This war on jihadism was aptly summed up by the Grand Imam of Al-Azhar, Dr. Ahmed El-Taiyeb, mainly in his speech before the Bundestag in Berlin in 2016. He referred to the jihadis as (my translation from the Arabic) **"the actions by a minority which claims its adherence to Islam. Their understanding of Islam is atrocious as they presented it to people everywhere as a faith of blood, whimsical to humanity, and destructive of civilizations."**

It is this novel approach to rediscovered wisdom which makes the NIRR a lethal weapon in confronting jihadism. For it denies not only its disturbed views. It attacks its very foundations as totally alien, totally beyond the pale, and hopelessly irredeemable.

CHAPTER 2

From Lofty Principles, Faulty Conclusions

It has been a slippery slope. From sky above at the inception of Islam in the 7th Century A.D., to mud below in ISIS, Al-Qaida, Al-Ansar, Boko Horam, Al-Shabab, and the renegade Muslim Brotherhood. These jihadi franchises have taken the texts of the Quran and of the Hadith of the Prophet Muhammad, and, without sanction or control, twisted them into an ideology of hate, murder, mayhem, targeting most of civilisation and humanity for annihilation. This has been a worldwide anti-civilization insurrection whose only hallmark was to make the words Islam and Muslims the equivalents of **"humanity's enemies No. One."**

The process took roots gradually. Every Muslim society in the 57th States whose majority population is Muslim, had its renegade groups. Their ostensible goal was **"the purification"** of Islam, first through non-authoritative **Fatwas** (non-enforceable religious advisory), ending up by the adoption of the sword as their logo or as the emblem on their national flags. The fact that the word **"sword"** was not mentioned even once in the Quran has been totally ignored.

The search for legitimating this world insurrection against faith and global security found in the political actions by non-Muslim powers against **"the Ummah"** (the Nation of Islam), including invasions, occupation and expropriation of national resources a galvanizing impetus. The extremists, acting in the midst of vast and largely uneducated masses, a fertile ground for support, funding, recruitment, and the fanciful claim to paradise in self-sacrifice. Thus their waging of **"jihad"** outside the clear bounds of Islamic law, and a tolerant Islamic culture and practice. **"Us Against Them"** became an accepted battle cry.

The conversion of the nascent Islamic democracy of the 7th and 8th centuries AD, through Shura (popular consultation), into a Byzantine style monarchical State was the starting point of that long and dreary fading away of the concept of Islam being a faith at home with other faiths. Though Islam does not create **"a State,"** but **"a community"** (Ummah), the State of the Umayyads of the late 7th century became an acceptable polity. It signaled **"the great schism."** That was between Medina, the capital of the first Islamic community, whose last leader was **Imam Ali Ibn Abi-Taleb,** the last of the four **"enlightened successors of Muhammad,"** and Damascus, the new imperial and debauched capital.

With this schism, which ended by the humiliation and assassination of Imam Ali, the cousin of Muhammad, the age of the true Caliphate was over. That is in spite of successive so-called Caliphates, rearing their heads nearly 14 centuries later. Such presumptive Caliphates led to ISIS (Daesh), headed by a thug from Al-Anbar, Iraq, by the name of Abu-Bakr Al-Baghdadi. In between, the rise of the Ottoman empire as of the 15th century, wielding the sword instead of the Islamic adage of **"You Have Your Faith, I Have Mine,"** signaled a seismic shift to non-Arab leadership of the Ummah. Force and military occupation of parts of the Balkans, as well as of parts of Arabia and populous Egypt, led to confrontations with Orthodox Christianity (mainly Russia) and to western collaboration to stop that kind of Islam.

Soon the Balkans and Egypt split away from Constantinople in the midst of the 19th century, leading eventually to the Turkish leader Ata-Turk renouncing the Caliphate in 1924, in order to focus on building up a truncated Turkey. With the Turkish yoke gone, nationalism, especially in Egypt and the Sudan, found in religion (Islam) a unifying factor. The Saudi State followed in 1932 led by King Abdul-Aziz, the founder of that State. But his success was shared with the Wahhabi movement -a body of thought which was far removed from the original intention of its founder in the 19th century.

By the middle of the 20th century, we have dark forces raising the deceptive flag of Islam that has no foundation in either the text of the Quran, or in the sayings and conduct of the Prophet Muhammad (the Sunna), or in the use of **"Hekmet"** (wisdom through common sense) which is one of the three pillars of an inclusive Islamic Law.

While Wahhabism denied, among other things, women their Islamic-based equality, it generously funded various extremist and arcane **"Islamic"** movements. Outside of Arabia, the national struggle found in supporting organizations, like **"The Muslim Brotherhood,"** a way of containing communism.

Egypt was the prime field for this zig-zagging between secularism, which has been an intrinsic DNA of Egypt for 7000 years, and the various Islamic **"movements"** including **"the Salafis"** -meaning the need to return to the purity of a very early Islam. Here it should be recalled that all these movements which falsely claimed the mantle of **"Islam"** had only one ideological framework in common: Religion is the easiest pathway to the psyche of a vast population whose majority cannot read, let alone get acquainted with Islam as a global culture.

Within that ferment of an imagined state versus faith, arose Bin Laden in the late 1990s from the womb of the real jihad against the Soviet invasion of Afghanistan. Between the Sudan, Somalia, and Afghanistan, Bin Laden, who had benefitted from western and Pakistani support during the military confrontation with the Soviet occupation of Afghanistan, found success in the ideological fog of the meaning of **"jihad."**

The primary salvo by Al-Qaida of which Bin Laden was the leader, was the destruction in 1998 of the American embassies in both Kenya and Tanzania. The success of that operation, and the tepid response to it by the U.S. under the Bill Clinton presidency, was a historic signal for the meticulous planning of the criminal attack of 9/11 on the U.S. America's reaction to 9/11, by invading Afghanistan in 2002, followed by the American war of choice on Iraq in 2003, represented the drawing of the battle lines between jihadism and the world response to it.

America, a close supporter of Israel in the face of the Palestinian struggle for a viable Arab State of their own, and with its military exposure in more than 100 countries, became a tempting target for jihadism. With America fighting its battle largely from the air, the least effective military posture for containing terrorism, the jihadi ground diverse groups stretching from the Philippines, across south-east Asia, to the Middle East, and westward to Africa, north and central, proved the struggle to be of long duration.

All the international conventions against terrorism, whether adopted by the League of Arab States (1998), the Conference of Islamic Cooperation (1999), or the UN (2000), proved to be only words on paper. The struggle was on: The response was derided by the jihadis as **"infidel aggression against Islam."**

Both the West and the jihadis had one characterization in common: lack of a unifying strategy on organization. Since 1998 till now, Sectarianism in Iraq, the brutal civil war in Syria since 2011, the Yemeni civil war, the fragmentation of Libya, have all proved to be disorienting signals for fighting jihadism by military force only. This is while Islamophobia in the US and Europe, accentuated by the flood of refugees from Muslim lands into non-Muslim countries, morphed, through the rise of the xenophobic right in America, France, the Netherland, and Scandinavia, into what is perceived today as **"a war against Islam."**

In the midst of these tectonic ideological movements, it became gradually clear that an ideological and robust response was needed to provide a rationale for the war on jihadism. The adoption of the secular Constitution of Egypt in 2014, followed by the election of Abdel-Fattah El-Sisi as president, signaled an institutional need for a **"New Islamic Religious Revolution."** Its goal was clear and its vehicle was a natural one -Al-Azhar.

The call by El-Sisi upon Al-Azhar to engage in and lead that new revolution were a real matching of need and historical resources. Al-Azhar response, under the iconic leadership of Sheikh Dr. Ahmed El-Taiyeb, a graduate of the Sorbonne (Paris) was massive. In more than a half a dozen presentations in Germany, Nigeria, France, Russia and the Arab world, El-Taiyeb provided the text and verse of that Revolution.

In waging that New Islamic Religious Revolution, Al-Azhar has a vast body of knowledge, resources, personnel and historic commitment to the Islam which jihadism has worked assiduously to debunk.

It reached through the deep past to pluck the diamonds from the deep troubled seas. A starting point was to remind the world how Islam, in its bright dawn of clarity, looked upon Christianity.

Here is an ideological pillar of this new revolution, represented by the pledge given by Omar, the 2nd Caliph after Muhammad, to the Christians of Jerusalem, following the Arab entry into northern Arabia. The text follows.

"We Pledge,
Security of person, finances, churches, crosses;
Security of the sick and the healthy and all their denominations;
Their churches shall not be made residential;
Their churches shall not be destroyed;
Their churches shall not be diminished in their value;
Their churches shall not be rezoned;

No funds or crosses shall be diminished;
Nor shall they be forced to convert;
Nor shall any of them be persecuted;
They shall only pay their property tax."
(My translation from the original Arabic).

To fully comprehend the ideological depth of Omar's pledge to the Christians in the Middle East, it should be juxtaposed with samples of what the terror franchises have done and advocated in the same region and beyond.

More importantly, some western academics, such as Graeme Wood of Yale University, have advanced erroneous claims regarding the ideological rise of ISIS. In his book **"The Way of the Strangers," Wood claims to have found jihadism to be rooted in** "the sacred texts, teachings and folklore of early Islam."[1]

Such egregious errors not only reflect ignorance of how Islam, born in the Arabian desert in the midst of vast tribal conflicts and practices (e.g. burying infant girls alive), has evolved. These claims could be read by jihadism as ideological justification for their criminality by myopic western scholarship.

For aside from the Quran and the conduct of the Prophet Muhammad (the Sunna), there exists a vast jurisdiction based on **"Hekmah"** (Reason; common sense), resting comfortably on the shoulders of ijtihad. It is called **"The non-textual jurisprudence."** For within the Quran of 6400 verses, there are no more than 200 verses which establish legal parameters. Thus the gaps created by **"non-texts"** are so vast, and the changing circumstances of life over 1400 years, have called for the application of **"Hekmah."**

This is a need alluded to by the Prophet Muhammad, on whose counsels women had a seat and a say. Moreover, Muhammad encouraged Ijmaa (consensus) as he said **"My Nation shall not reach a consensus based on falsehood."**

The New Islamic Religious Revolution does not confront only the gross errors adopted by terrorist organizations in interpreting Islam to fit in with

---

[1] Quoted from Dexter Filkins, "On the Fringes of ISIS," <u>The New York Times Book Review</u>, January 22, 2017, page 13.

their criminal purposes. It also aims at responding to the misconceptions about Islam reflected in the writings and media opinions of western and other authors.

Examples of this latter category abound. But high on that list is **Bernard Lewis** of Princeton (in his **"What Went Wrong"**) and **Ayaan Hirsi Ali** (in her **"Infidel," "The Caged Virgin,"** and other books.)

Among the reasons these two authors head that list is that they have no excuse in not being able to understand or read the Arabic language, a primary requirement for becoming intimately acquainted with the Quran and the Hadith.

The error by Lewis lies mainly in his calling for **"the reformation"** of Islam a la Martin Luther. Through ijtihad and the resort to the **"public interest jurisdiction,"** Islam has been in constant adjustment to changing circumstances. A faulty assumption leads to another. Thus Lewis reaches an unsupported conclusion about a **"clash between Islam and modernity in the Middle East."** Here his error lies in his confusing between what Islam calls for and how it is practiced.

As to **Hirsi Ali,** her errors, contrary to those of Lewis, are animus-based. Her Somali tribal and non-Islamic practices, especially in regard to genital mutilation and forced betrothment, are blamed by her on Islam itself. She even goes to the limit of calling for a revision of the Quran. Islamic dogma, which she totally missed, is that the Quran was not authored. It was revealed. Opting out of Islam is her personal choice. But confusing between the tribal pre-Islamic practices of her country of origin (Somalia) amounts to opportuning a global environment ready to unjustly punish Islam for terrorism.

Obviously, it is not my intention to respond to all adversarial sources which do injustice to the precepts of mainstream Islam. Were this to be attempted, it would take volumes to do so. The present confrontation is only targeting the hallucinatory preaching for killing and destruction adopted by ISIS, Al-Qaida, and the like. All within the context of warring on that ideology by a counter ideology -a weapon which until now has not been sufficiently raised, let alone used.

What makes this study rather timely is that its appearance coincides with the age of Trumpism in America. It has been abundantly clear that Trumpism sees jihadism as Islamism.

In his inaugural speech of Jan. 20, 2017, Donald Trump said: The US would **"unite the civilized world against radical Islamic terrorism which we will eradicate completely from the face of the earth."**

In this regard, Trump manifested a thesis which has the unintended value of bolstering jihadism. There is no **"radicalism"** in Islam; terrorism has no association with any recognizable faith; world unity should be based on the bedrock value of cooperation in constructive endeavors, not on only warring upon terrorist franchises.

Moreover, Trump is also advised by a National Security Advisor, Lieutenant General MIchael Flynn, (now gone) who has declared Islam to be **"a cancer."** Such epithets can only favor the criminal ideology of terrorism under the assumed name of Islam. Giving aid and comfort to jihadism have now come in the form of **"war on Islam"** itself. This is what ISIS and its cohorts have been advocating, especially in the 9/11 period, as tools for legitimation, funding, recruitment, and raison d'etre.

It is regrettable that the repeated Trumpist savaging of Islam has so far escaped the label of **"hate speech,"** an actionable offense.

Yet it has been used as a launching pad for another weird claim by Trump. **"We will eradicate ("Islamic Terrorism") completely from the faith of the earth."** For its ultimate success, the war on jihadism should be perceived as an existential battle of long duration. It is not only an American war; it is a war in which a multitude of States have to be involved each in its own way, by its own means, through its own sovereign obligation. It cannot be seen as a war in which America is the decider and the banner-holder. For the wars in Afghanistan and Iraq have demonstrated the folly of invading Muslim countries, en masse, in pursuit of inarticulate objectives (sometimes faulty, as in the case of the fiction of Saddam's possession of weapons of mass destruction.)

The continuing drum-beat by Trump against the misperceived menace of Islam as a faith for 1.7 billion people must be music to the ears of jihadism. For in the 5th day of his presidency, he has coined the ominous new label - **"terror prone nations."** That was in the context of his threatened **"crackdown on immigrants and bolster(ing) national security, including slashing the number of refugees who can resettle in the United States."[2]**

---

[2] Natana J. Delong-Bas, <u>Wahhabi Islam: From Revival and Reform to Global Jihad</u> (New York and London: Oxford University Press, 2004), p.124.

The essential lesson to be learnt in warring on jihadism ideologically, is the need for inter-state coordination, especially in the area of intelligence gathering, avoiding in the process even the resemblance of outside intervention. Such an approach may also be fitting for the new Trump call for letting countries defend themselves, or pay for buying defense from the U.S.

CHAPTER 3

Gender Inequality: A Tribal Fabrication

Western scholarship has focused attention on gender inequality in Islam. It is ironic to find that Islam, at of its birth, has liberated women through giving them a status equal to that of men. That was nearly a thousand years before women in Europe were freed from being mere chattel -movable possessions. The fact cannot be ignored that Islamic practices in most Muslim majority countries subverted gender equality. That is while women in western societies were climbing the ascendancy ladder to gender equality.

Yet such discrepancy between Islamic law and its application would be totally injurious to the fact that Islamic jurisprudence in several States has remedied that discrepancy through legislation. This is with the exception of countries like Saudi Arabia which, through the sway of Wahhabism, has adhered to a literal and archaic interpretation of Islam. In amplification, it should be stated that the originator of Wahhabism Muhammad Ibn Abdel-Wahhab had adhered to an interpretation of Islam which was totally different from that adopted by the movement which later carried his name.

In her seminal study of entitled **"Wahhabi Islam: From Revival and Reform to Global Jihad (2014),"** Natana J. Delong-Bas, fully delineated the chasm between Ibn Abdel-Wahhab and Wahhabism, the latter being an oppressive theocracy. With regard to the issue of gender in public life, she states the following: **"The overall image of women in his works is based on an appreciation of human life and the human condition in which women are viewed as divinely created people, who not only have a part to play in the process of salvation in the afterlife, but are also expected to play an active role in this life in the establishment of**

an Islamic order on earth in both the private and public realms." [3]

How deep is the ravine separating between the espousal by Ibn Abdel-Wahhab of gender equality and the dark practices in today's Saudi Arabia. This includes total segregation between the sexes; limitation of the professions which Saudi women can engage in; deprivation of licensing to drive a car, or to appear in court as an attorney; and the prohibition on travel unless accompanied by a male mentor of the woman's immediate family.

And how distinct is this gender-based apartheid in Saudi Arabia, the custodian of the holy places of **Mecca** and **Medina,** from the practices in countries like Egypt, Jordan, Tunisia, Turkey, Iraq or Lebanon. In Egypt, for example, women are trained and licensed to be aircraft pilots and police officers. The same is true with other countries where they sit in legislature chambers as law-makers!!

This diversity of practices contributed to the rise of Al-Qaida, ISIS and similar terror organizations, luring, for example young women to join them in jihadism in various lands. That included the heinous industry of prostitution by jihadis under the misleading label of **"jihadi fornication"** - sex with several men as a means of lustful comfort.

In the midst of all these confusing approaches to the standing of women as equals to men looms now a definitive assurance of that equality. This is undoubtedly a veritable ideological weapon against jihadism because it flows from the Quran, the Hadith, and the amplification of these primary legal sources by Al-Azhar as a citadel of Islamic learning.

Providing for both the economic independence of women and their parity with men, the Quran states: **"To men a share for what they have earned, and to women a share for what they have earned."** (Chapter IV, Verse 32). Guarding against illegal sequestering by men of women's material possession, the Quran, in an earlier verse in the same Chapter cited above, stresses: **"... and do not constrain them so that you may take some of what you have given them." (verse 19).**

In Sharia, as primarily based on the Quran, women inherit half of what an inheriting male receives. In verse 176 of the same Chapter, it states: **"If a**

---

[3] The Grand Imam Mahmoud Shaltout, <u>Islam: Faith and Law</u> (Cairo: Dar Al-Shrooq, Cairo, 2015), pp 208-209 (21st edition).

person dies childless and leaves behind a sister, she shall get half of his inheritance." For this inequality in inheritance, there is a historic reason, and a modern remedy. At the time of Islam's inception, women were exempt from combat (though they opted for participation), and their male folks were the economic pillar of the family. However, in several Muslim countries, modern legislation has remedied that inequality wherever possible. That has been mainly accomplished through legislation, wills and estate planning. That process has accelerated due to women ascending to membership of legislatures and other positions of secular political power.

Raising the voice for gender equality in Islam, the Grand Imam of Al-Azhar, Dr. Ahmed El-Taiyeb, told the German Bundestag in Berlin on March 15, 2016: **"In Sharia, women are men's full partners in rights and obligations. Muhammad, the Prophet of Islam, declared that women are equal to men."** **The marginalization of women in the East is not due to Islam's precepts. This perception is far from the truth. The fact is that that marginalization is due to adherence to worn out traditions and customs which have nothing to do with Islam."**

An earlier Grand Imam of Al-Azhar, Sheikh Mahmoud Shaltout, declared unequivocally gender equality in Islam. In his book, **"Islam: Faith and Law,"** he cited how a woman (Khawlah Bint Thaalab) argued on an equal basis with Muhammad and won. In contesting the validity of her husband declaring her divorced, Khawlah won that argument hands down. The Quran includes a whole chapter on this historic episode (Chapter 58).

The first verse of that chapter, entitled **"The Discussion,"** meaning **"the argument,"** states: **"God has indeed heard the saying of she who discusses with you about her husband, and she complains to God. And God hears your conversion, surely God is All-Hearing, All-Seeing."**

Commenting on this Quranic depiction of gender equality, Sheikh Shaltout says: **"See how has God elevated the status of women, respected her views, and placed her at par with God's Messenger. Thus her (Khawlah's) view became Sharia forever ... Such an episode is nothing short of an eternally valid evidence over the length of time. It reflected Islam's respect for women's opinions."**[4]

Sheikh Shaltout also brought up women's role in combat. Quoting from **Al-**

---

[4] <u>Ibid.</u>, p. 209.

Bokhary, one of the main repositories of authenticated Hadith by the Prophet Muhammad, he quoted from one of the women's companions of Muhammad saying: **"We participated with God's Messenger in his (defensive) wars -providing the combatants with water and other services, and evacuating the dead and injured to Al-Medinah (the first capital of Islam)."**

The author, Imam Shaltout, concludes: **"Therefore, the need calls for women to ready themselves for these duties, by learning nursing and other services needed by the armed services as among the responsibilities which suit her female status with a view to perfecting the rendering of these duties in combat."[5]**

What a far cry from the Wahhabism of today which relegates most women to walled enclosures. Alternately, how far removed from the truth about gender equality under Islam are the false claims made by Donald Trump, Michael Flynn, Steve Bannon and other US recently-elevated leaders!!

There is nothing in Sharia (Islamic Law) that compels a female to marry against her will. In her book, **Heretic,** Ayaan Hirsi Ali, superimposing her irrelevant Somali tribal background on Sharia, states: **"When I arrived in the Netherland, I feared that my father or his clansmen or the man I had been assigned to marry, would simply appear and force me to submit against my will. When the Dutch officials told me that there were laws to protect me and that the Netherlands would not recognize my arranged marriage because it has no legal standing, I marveled at this system, so different from the Islamic code."[6]**

The fact of the matter is that **"the Islamic code"** does not recognize forced marriages. When Hirsi Ali describes Somalia's pre-Islamic tribal traditions as **"The Sharia Paradox,"** she injures Sharia multiple times: Somalia might be Islamic by name only, but pre-Islamic by practice; Hirsi's flight to the Netherlands due to her ignorance of Sharia has fed into the cacophony of Islamophobia; and Hirsi's constant pursuit in four of her books in those misguided attacks has lionized her materially thus making of hate a profitable industry.

------

[5] Ibid., p. 210.

[6] Ayaan Hirsi Ali, Heretic: Why Islam Needs a Reformation Now (New York: Harper Collins, 2015), pp. 141-142.

From Muhammad's days, Islamic law has made of marriage a contract, with woman a free agent to choose. Her right to have her own wealth could not be derogated by depriving her from choosing her life partner. On this fulcrum point of gender equality, Imam Shaltout offers multiple evidence on women's freedom to choose. Arguing for what he describes as **"Women's Rights In a Marriage Contract,"** he wonders loudly: **"How can a woman's male decider possess the right to force her to marry someone she doesn't like …? Undoubtedly a woman's self is close to her than her material possessions!! How would a woman feel if she were to be deprived of having a say about her very life by taking away her freedom to contract in marriage?"**[7]

That Grand Imam of Al-Azhar does not stop there. He cites a precedent by Muhammad (a Sunna -part of the true Islamic code). Upon a complaint by a woman (Khansa Bint Jozam) that her father forced upon her a marriage against her will, Muhammad promptly annulled that forced marriage.[8]

In yet another precedent, a house maid complained to Muhammad that her father imposed his will upon her to marry someone against her will, Muhammad gave her a post-marital choice: nullification or personal acceptance. She chose the latter. Her choice is the heart of **"the Islamic code."** She said: **"I only wanted to teach women that their parents have no say in their marriage choice."**[9]

The Hirsi discovery of the Dutch code giving her that freedom might have been a revelation to her because of her tribal pre-Islamic environment. Thus her call for **"A Reformation Now"** for Islam has no place in Islamic law wherever it is properly applied. Measuring Islamic law's keeping up with the times by the least informed environment about its sources (The Quran, the Hadith, and the public good jurisdiction) is decidedly a faulty measure.

It is also noteworthy that in regard to the nullification of an undesirable marriage, outside intervention is unnecessary. The examples cited above had the Prophet Muhammad as the agent for nullification. Yet the protection given by Islamic Law to the primacy of choice by the aggrieved married wife includes the initiation by women of divorce unilaterally.

---

[7] Shaltout, op. Cit., p. 213.

[8] Ibid., p. 214.

[9] Id.

By doing so, the fullness of gender equality is plain for all to see. This method of marriage dissolution by action initiated by the female spouse is called **"Khulu."** This Arabic word may be translated as **"the shedding of a burden."** To effect khulu, whose practice began since the inception of Islam, has been the return by the wife of the dowery by which her husband has betrothed her.[10]

Thus in Khulu, the dissolution of marriage is predicated upon an initiative by a wife seeking an out from an unwanted marriage. Aside from the return of the dowery, its other requirement is seeking that termination before a judge. Judicial approval is assured through the wife's returning of the dowry to her divorced husband.

To study **"The New Islamic Religious Revolution"** as a lethal weapon against Jihadism requires, in my view, depth of knowledge of the Arabic language. This is central to the understanding of the huge diversity of Muslim geography, an accurate measurement of the chasm between Islamic law and its practices in a variety of regions, and an ability to interpret this combination of factors, including modern legislation, through appropriate reading.

Setting forth those standards, we find western interpreters of Sharia (Islamic Law) have mostly failed to meet them. Bernard Lewis is such an example. In his book (a New York Times Bestseller) entitled **"What Went Wrong,"** he makes this affirmation:
"According to Islamic law and tradition, there were three groups of people who did not benefit from the general Muslim principle of legal and religious equality -unbelievers, slaves, and women. The woman was obviously, in one significant respect, the worst-placed of the three."[11]

Such a nudum factum assertion by Professor Lewis is unbelievable in view of the fact that he ris familiar with Arabic. As to unbelievers, the subsequent chapter of this book shall be addressing it. Regarding slavery, historical evidence shows that both east and west have engaged in it in one

---

[10] Muhammad Naguib Awadain Al-Mughrabi, <u>Al-Khulu</u> (Cairo: Dar Al-Nahdha Al-Arabiah, 2006), p. 8 (In Arabic)

[11] Bernard Lewis, <u>What Went Wrong? The Clash Between Islam and Modernity in the Middle East</u> (New York: Harper Collins, 2002), p. 67.

form or another.

In Arabia, slavery was an integral part of the socio-economic scene. In Islam, from its beginning, had a direct impact on collapsing that practice. This has been accomplished through various methods: religious injunction, economic reward to the liberators of slaves, intermarriage between slave and free, and the drafting of slaves into military service (e.g. The Mamluks, who later ruled over Egypt until 1805).

There are no examples supported by religious text or legal sanction for the kind of enslavement seen in the Americas by whites of blacks. A look at the faces of millions of pilgrims to Mecca and Medina reflects a huge panorama of all colors of humans, Such multitudes are seen standing shoulder to shoulder, prostrating themselves, not before a human master, but before their one Creator.

There is a valid reason for Muslims to say: **"Sharia is for every time and every place."** This has been translated in the west into a threat of forcing **"Sharia"** onto non-Muslim societies. That unfounded fear approaches insanity for more than one reason. First: How can you force a legal system upon geographic areas where you do not physically occupy them by military means? Second: There are today no Muslim armies in occupation of any non-Muslim countries. The reverse is true. Third: The outcome of this unfounded fear, whose roots are nourished by Islamophobia, is that in America, several States have legislated a ban on even mentioning the word **"Sharia"** in their State courts. General Michael Flynn, the former national security advisor of President Trump has repeatedly warned America about Islam, which he does not regard as a faith but as an ideology. He falsely claims that Muslims intend to force Sharia upon America!!

Yet the meaning of the relevance of Sharia to every time and place is due to its keeping its adaptability to changing circumstances. This is done through two ways: **ijtihad** (more on that in later chapters), and legislation with which we deal now, especially in the context of gender equality.

Taking, as an example, the secular Constitution of Egypt of 2014, we find Article Eleven begins by: **"The State guarantees equality between women and men in all spheres of civil, political, economic, social and cultural rights in accordance with the provisions of the Constitution."** Then it goes on to deal with the State's responsibility for adopting all measures which **"guarantee for women appropriate representation in legislative councils."**

Such guarantees also extend to women assumption of public service positions, high administrative posts, employment in judicial establishments, with no discrimination against her because of gender.

All basic laws flow from constitutions. The aforementioned Constitution, which is the legal framework for one-third of the Arab world which is called Egypt, is not the only such fundamental law in the other 21 of 57 States making up the Organization of Islamic Cooperation.

There are also more universal legal frameworks which have conditioned Sharia for being relevant to changing circumstances. Preeminent among these are the Charter of the United Nations of 1945[12], (a treaty to which all Arab and Muslim States subscribe); the Universal Declaration of Human Rights of 1948, and all United Nations conventions adopted for the past more than 70 years. Of special importance among these are the 1966 UN Conventions on Civil and Political Rights, and on Economic and Social Rights.

Adherence to such international instruments not only bestow on the subscribing States their legitimacy. It also creates universalism for the Rule of Law which makes the violations of these provisions actionable matters which may lead to sanctions and even, in cases of severity, charges of war crimes.

The Islamic stamp of approval of such principles and legal foundations has been added in several documents made public by Al-Azhar, with the endorsement of the Coptic Church. This is particularly so in the document of June 19, 2011. Consisting of eleven principles, this document declares: **"Commitment to the institutional structure relative to basic freedoms for thought and expression, with complete adherence to human rights, women rights, and the rights of the child."**

This is an integrated fabric which, in the case of Islamic law as it applies to gender equality, joins together that equality, with the religious text of the Quran, the Sunna of Muhammad, the jurisdiction of the public good, and the universality of the Rule of Law. To claim gender inequality under Islam is nothing but a total lack of understanding of what today's Religious Revolution is all about.

---

[12] The preamble of the UN Charter included "promoting and encouraging respect for human rights and for fundamental freedoms of all without distinction as to race, sex, language, or religion" (Article 1, para. 3).

It is indeed shameful to have in Wahhabi Saudi Arabia of today a woman posting on Twitter a plea -a sign in front of her face. It read: **"I am a prisoner and my crime is that I'm a Saudi woman."** Another Saudi woman, Moudi al-Johani, 26, said, following gaining asylum in the U.S., that her family had locked her up when she returned from Florida during a college vacation. In 2016, Moudi fled to America and joined online campaigners who started #StopEnslavingSaudiWomen.[13]

---

[13] The New York Times, April 23, 2017, p. A7. An article titled: "With Daring Cellphone Videos, Saudi Women Are Challenging Male Control."

CHAPTER 4

One-ness of God Is Equality Among Faiths

"Allahu Akbar" (God is Great) has been misunderstood for a battle cry by Muslims confronting adherents of other faiths. Far from it. It means **"we are all equal before God regardless of any faith we hold."** Only the jihadis hold to the mistaken interpretation, not only against non-Muslims, but also against Muslims who do not share their distorted interpretation of Islam.

Here the Quran gives clear evidence. In Chapter 42, Verse 13, we read: **"He has ordained for you the Religion which He commanded to Noah, and that we have revealed to you, and that which He commanded to Abraham, and Moses, and Jesus: 'Establish the Religion, and be not divided therein.'"**

Interpreting these words to his Nigerian audience in Abuja, in May 2016, Imam Dr. El-Taiyeb of Al-Azhar said: **"Whatever was ordained before Islam remains sacred unless repealed by text thereafter."**[14]

Again Dr. El-Taiyeb quoted from the Quran (Chapter 5, Verse 46), where it states: **"And We sent following in their footsteps, Jesus the son of Mary, confirming what was before him of the Torah, and We gave him the Scriptures in which guidance and light, and confirming what was before it of the Torah, and a guidance and an admonition for the pious."**

---

[14] Translated from the Arabic text of Dr. El-Taiyeb's statement in Abuja, May 2016.

It thus becomes evident that the New Islamic Religious Revolution, in its war on jihadism, is intent on confronting the unislamic nature of that cult in more than one way: it attacks jihadism illusory barriers between one faith and the other; it makes of all faiths a continuum which is uninterrupted by geography, language, color, or belief; it reminds of the universality of Islam as a link in a global chain of faith; and it rejects the apartheid hierarchy which propels jihadism towards the notion that Islam is superior to other faiths.

Once more we return to Al-Azhar's Grand Imam as he declares before the German Bundestag: **"Islam is linked to revealed religions by an organic link which is unbreakable. For we, Muslims, believe that both the Torah, the New Testament, and the Quran are guidance and light to all peoples. The later faith confirms its predecessor."**

He went on to say: Our faith in either the Quran or Muhammad cannot be perfected without our belief in these earlier revealed religions. We read in the Quran: **"Surely, those who believe (Muslims) and the Jews, and the Nasarah (those who followed Jesus's true message) and the Sabians (monotheists) whosoever believes in God and the Last Day and performs deeds of righteousness, they shall have their reward with their Lord, no fear shall be on them, nor shall they grieve"** (Chapter 2, Verse 62).

This is a far cry from the jihadist propaganda about **"the other."** It is also quite removed from the declarations made by the Trumpists and others who had adopted the jihadi language and terminology. Those declarations epitomized **"fake news."** They fancied the Islamic creed a real threat to the security of America and beyond. This is evidenced by Trump's executive order banning Muslim citizens from six predominantly Muslim countries. A precipitous move which flies in the face of the U.S. Constitution's First Amendment as well as due process.

That one-ness of God is a cardinal principle of the new Islamic revolution for reasons beyond religious faith. It touches upon several central issues of primary importance to vanquishing jihadism. Its luminous rays extend to: (i) the importance of global dialogue; (ii) the primacy of human dignity; (iii) the smooth integration of Muslim newcomers in Europe and elsewhere within a globalized culture; (iv) it highlights diversity as a feature of inter-cultural interaction; and (v) it makes of freedom of belief an ideological mechanism for a peaceful existence.

An elaboration of the five precepts mentioned above, as separate items, might take away from their inter-relatedness. Thus the following analysis shall take all of them as one multi-faceted quantum **stressing the importance of the one-ness of God.** In his statement before the Bundestag in mid-March 2016, Imam El-Taiyeb took his cue directly from the words of the Quran.

The Quran unambiguously states: **"If God had so willed, He would have made you a single nation, but (His plan is) to test you in what He has given you: so strive to vie with one another in good deeds; to God is the return of all of you, and He will tell you the truth of the matters in which you differe."**[15]

Aligning the Quranic Verse with the central thesis of the Islamic revolution, the Grand Imam of Al-Azhar shared with the German Parliament the following: **"Diversity among people, and the differences between them in their nature are fully acknowledged in the Quran. Thus the Quran built on that diversity the law of international relations in Islam and called it 'getting to know you.' These ideas, per force, require dialogue, not only with those with whom we agree, but also with those with whom we disagree. And this is what our present world needs in order to overcome its suffocating crises."**[16]

The conclusion by the Grand Imam was crisp: **"It is therefore difficult for a Muslim to imagine pouring all peoples, nations, in one religion and in one culture."**[17] Hence, the huge gulf between Islamic jurisprudence and the lunatic advocacy by ISIS and those who adhere to the Trumpist notion that all Muslims, in their search for dominance, think alike.

It is saddening to have to link between jihadism and Trumpism. But the thrust of their respective propaganda to the outside world is mutually reinforcing. Whether wittingly or unwittingly, Trumpism is giving ISIS the verbal tools of war on Islam. No better igniters of jihadism can be found.

As to **"human dignity"** in Islamic jurisprudence, it is abbreviated in the

---

[15] The Quran, Chapter 5, Verse 48.

[16] From the statement in Arabic by Dr. El-Taiyeb before the Bundestag in Berlin on March 15, 2016.

[17] Id.

term **"justice."** Listed in the Quran 28 times, the word **"ADL,"** in Arabic meaning justice, is even one of the 99 names given God Himself.

The Quranic words are: **"When you judge between man and man, that you judge with justice."**[18] This is a signature phrase appearing on the wall behind every judge's bench throughout the Muslim world. It is the equivalent in America of **"In God We Trust."** If, as in many instances, it is more observed in the breach, especially through dictatorship and Wahhabism, the negative phenomenon cannot be blamed on the faith itself.

The UN Chapter, though a World War II document, made **"the dignity and worth of the human person"** a part of its preamble.[19] The rise of the Right in Europe and America has been propelled, not to a small degree, by the flood of Muslim refugees not accepting cultural integration. Those seemingly unassimilable throngs suffered a backlash, particularly with regard to the perception in the West of Islam. **"Stop the Islamization of Europe,"** rose a cry which resonated with millions. Weaponizing these European sentiments, Trumpism made a Muslim ban the equivalent of a cultural high wall whose purpose, to quote Donald Trump, was **"to get our country back."**

Addressing this issue, the Quran phrases it in the context of justice towards non-Muslims. **"God forbids you not, with regard to those who have not fought you in the cause of Religion, nor expelled you from your homes, that you should be considerate and deal justly with them; surely God loves the just."**[20] Building on that, the Grand Imam of Al-Azhar said in Berlin in March 2016: **"I wish that every Muslim who now lives in Europe would put this verse in a beautiful frame and place it in his office or in his store, or in his cell. This would be a permanent reminder that fairness is the apex of good morality … Justice and gratitude are integral parts of the attitude of Muslims towards others. This same treatment should be extended to any brother in humanity."**

Compare these guidelines presented by the Quran, as interpreted by Al-Azhar's Grand Imam, to Daesh's untiring attempts to smuggle terrorists

---

[18] <u>The Quran</u>, Chapter 4, Verse 58.

[19] The UN Charter, Preamble.

[20] <u>The Quran</u>, Chapter 60, Verse 8.

within the human wave of refugees heading toward Europe. Theirs is a nihilistic ideology which found in Islam a convenient cover from which to wage jihadist mischief in the name of God!!

When it comes to diversity and its connectedness to freedom of belief, we find these two elements acting as code words for a peaceful co-existence. There is nothing in the jihadi mythology that can point up to the importance of diversity being the other side of the coin of the freedom of belief. One does not have to search hard for the reasons for that ideological nonsense in jihadism. For the jihadi bubble keeps all notions of faith globalization out of its dark orbit. To terror organizations, the so-called religious purity in the sense of Sunni selectivity is their oxygen for survival.

By contrast, the Abuja statement by Dr. El-Taiyeb made in May 2016, collapses those strange notions as inimical to the New Islamic Religious Revolution. He said: **"This Al-Azhar visit has come to you to emphasize to all sectors of the noble Nigerian people that Islam is a humanitarian faith, a faith standing for security and peace, regionally and globally."**[21] Then he pointedly added: **"Never, not even for one day, has Islam been an advocacy for violence, killing, orphans-creator, or for catastrophe befalling peaceful citizens day in and day out."** Of course, such declarations were specifically pointing to Boko Haram, the young women snatchers, who have for years defied Nigeria's law and order in its northeast.

Then the Grand Imam of Al-Azhar cited a Quranic warning to those marauders: **"And do not think that God is unaware of what the wrongdoers do. He only puts them in respite until a Day when eyes shall stare"** (meaning the Day of Judgement).[22]

In the universalization of faith, the one-ness of God, as a basic concept, permeates the new religious revolution. **"Wahid"** (Arabic for One) occurs in the Quran no less than 30 times. Muhammad, in one of his authenticated Hadiths (sayings) declared: **"I have the primary privilege to belong to Jesus, son of Mary, here on earth and in the hereafter. The prophets are brothers, though from different mothers. Their faith is one."**[23]

---

[21] El-Taiyeb Abuja Declaration, May 2016, <u>op. cit.</u>

[22] <u>The Quran</u>, Chapter 14, Verse 42.

[23] As quoted by Dr. El-Taiyeb in his speech in Abuja. <u>Op. Cit.</u>

Though one globalized faith, the laws derived from each of them vary from place to place. In revealed religions, Abraham is **"the father"** -the originator, for whom a whole chapter in the Quran (Chapter 14) is devoted by name. The non-revealed religions, such as Hinduism, Buddhism and Confucianism, are also included in that concept of **"one-ness"** by extension. For the main thread is not **"faith"** standing alone, but **"faith"** as an expression of humanity, which is relationally governed by **"kindness and fairness."**[24]

Note should be taken here that the Quran advises not only Muslims. It generally addresses **"Al-Insan"** (The human being.) Throughout the Quran, this term occurs in many places. It reflects the essential fact that, contrary to what the Muslim Brotherhood and other organizations which trade in faith advocate, Islam did not create a State. It created an **"Ummah"** -a community of human beings linked together by a variety of faiths. Thus **"one-ness"** and diversity are in effect the two sides of the same human coin.

These concepts which are advanced by the New Islamic Religious Revolution seem to have gone unnoticed by the Trump administration. Trump's former National Security Advisor, Lt. General Michael Flynn has advocated a completely dark narrative. In his book **"The Field of Fight,"** he warns: **"We're in a world war against a messianic mass movement of evil people, most of them inspired by a totalitarian ideology: Radical Islam."**[25] So instead of focusing on organizations and individuals intent on terrorizing America and the rest of the world, the Trumpists are looking upon all Muslims as the enemy.

Quoting from Trump during the campaign of 2016, we find him saying: **"I think Islam hates us."**[26] A Trumpist, by the name of Sebastian Gorka, national security editor at the ultra-right website Breitbart News, is also the author of a book titled **"Defeating Jihad."** In it, he characterizes **"radical Islam"** as a grave threat as Hitler was in World War II and the Soviet Union in the Cold War.[27]

---

[24] Id.

[25] As quoted in The New York Times, January 26, 2017, p. A28.

[26] Id.

[27] Id.

It is to be expected that such unenlightened approaches to jihadism are bound to fail. Defeating jihadism is not by military force alone. Terrorist ideology needs to be also confronted by a counter ideology. And this is what the New Islamic Religious Revolution provides.

Cutting off the Muslim world from partnering in the war on jihadism is a recipe for failure. For it chokes off the flow of information necessary to vanquish terrorism from the variety of Muslim cultures. In anti-jihadism, there is no substitute for human credible intelligence and advocacy. Islam is a central component of that defensive mix, and calling jihadism **"Islamic terrorism"** makes that mix far from assimilable. Jihadism, which is terrorism by any other name, has no faith.

There is no question that terrorism has been a primary cause for hate of Islam and Muslims by the non-Muslim world. Terrorism has been a blotch on the name of Islam and has augmented ignorance of what Islam as a faith is all about. The new religious revolution is now trying to fill this huge gap between fact and fiction. Its new counter-attack against jihadism, which is not yet fully comprehended worldwide, is advancing through several ideological platforms, including the platform of the one-ness of God.

In his speech in Paris, in June 2016, the Grand Imam of Al-Azhar, cogently elaborated upon several of these conceptual platforms. Addressing the Second Dialogue Encounter Between the Eastern and Western Wise Leaders, Dr. El-Taiyeb called for the adoption of **"universality"** (Aalamiyah) as a replacement of **"globalization"** (Aawlamiah). There is a subtle but important difference between the two approaches to the idea of world cooperation.[28] While globalization calls for cultural and civilizational fusion, universality calls for integration, which we find to be the Canadian model. Integration sees no problem in the espousal by a migrant of the new host culture while keeping the absorbable elements of the native culture of that migrant.

Muslim refugees flooding non-Muslim countries, look upon fusion as costing them the loss of their native values and identities. By contrast, integration, when properly prepared for and applied, those values and identities which the migrants and refugees carry with them to the west are kept in harmony with the new cultures of the host lands.

---

[28] El-Taiyeb's statement in Arabic in Paris in June 2016.

In that context, Dr. El-Taiyeb issued in Paris the following call: **"I propose for our next Dialogue the topic of 'positive integration.' Therefore, I call upon the Muslim citizens in Europe to realize that they are now bona fide citizens in their new communities. Such citizenship does not negate an integration which safeguards their religious identity."**

Citing the historic **"Medina Document,"** promulgated by the Prophet Muhammad following his migration (hijrah) from Mecca to Medina, fleeing from persecution in Mecca, the Grand Imam of Al-Azhar described it in these words: **"It was the first Constitution known to humanity as it set forth the principle of equality in rights and obligations amongst inhabitants who were diverse in faith and ethnicity."**[29]

He went on to nullify the existence of substantial contradictions between some European legislation and Islamic law. In this context, the Imam of Al-Azhar bemoaned political isolation imposed by Muslims upon themselves due to what they perceive as contradiction. **"Such laws,"** he reasoned, are not forcefully imposed by the State for the purpose of negating Islamic law. Whenever this happens, the aggrieved Muslims may resort to appeal from their effect. For now is the time to move from the jurisdiction for **"minorities,"** to the jurisdiction for integration and inter-active co-existence.[30]

These are the essential ideological junctures in the concept of **"The Oneness of God."** It is a strong bridge to every faith and creed. It is also an anchor in the new religious revolution which advocates that all faiths, regardless of their ritualistic context or their externalities, are equal. Establishing a faith hierarchy of importance or of credibility, is a denial of faith itself.

The whole thesis of the New Islamic Religious Revolution resonates with the preface of the constitution of the UN Educational, Scientific, and Cultural Organization (UNESCO). As the Religious Revolution envisages fighting the destructive ideology of jihadism with its own constructive ideology, we find a parallel in these words of UNESCO's constituent instrument: **"Since wars begin in the minds of men, it is in the minds of men that the defences of peace must be constructed."**

---

[29] <u>Id.</u>

[30] <u>Ibid.</u>

CHAPTER 5

Takfir (Apostasy) As A Jihadi Sledge-Hammer

Apostasy (In Arabic: Takfir) is an abandonment of a previous loyalty or a defection from a previous faith. This form of renunciation has been made a central tenet by the jihadis and, in many cases, non-jihadis, as a non-forgivable defection. Punishment for that defection is death **as decreed by them.** Declaring someone to be an apostate (Kafir) is nothing short of religious fascism. It is frequently used by jihadis as a weapon sanctioning extra-judicial killing.

The Quran is on point in denying apostasy advocates that legitimacy. **"There is no compulsion in Religion."**[31] This principle permeates the entire new Islamic religious revolution which is returning Islam to its ideological roots: **"freedom of choice."** The term **"unholy"** is an orientalist term, which does not exist in Islamic jurisprudence.

The crime of Takfirism stems from having a human being hurling at another a false judgement which interferes with the direct relationship between every human being and God. Thus apostasy is a form of usurpation of a power -the power to judge the quality of faith -which can only be left to the hereafter. That was the implication of what Sheikh Ahmed El-Taiyeb said in his Bundestag speech. **"Religion has to be comprehended only through the heavenly directives and the practices of the Prophet who conveyed them to their publics."**[32] None of these Takfiris can be regarded as an interpreter of these directives or practices.

---

[31] <u>The Quran</u>, Chapter 2, Verse 256.

[32] Dr. El-Taiyeb, Speech before the Bundestag, Berlin, March 15, 2016.

The same theme is once again reflected, though in a different way, in the statement by Sheikh Al-Azhar in **Abuja, Nigeria in May 2016.** Referring to the all-encompassing view of humanity in the Quran, he said: **"The Quran views all individuals as equal to one another. They are the progeny of one father and one mother. Here, therefore, we have a human unity, where individuals get to know one another. Amongst them, there is no preferential hierarchy, except for the performance of good deeds."**

Those utterances have solid support in the Quran as regards which people should not be subjected to enmity. **"God forbids you not with regard to those who have not fought you in the cause of Religion, nor expelled you from your homes, that you should be considerate and deal justly with them; surely God loves the just."**[33] Only in self defense in the context of armed conflict, could a sector of humanity be excluded, or slandered, or persecuted. In none of these acts, is Takfirism (apostasy) to be regarded as innocent Muslim practice.

A case in point is that of **Omar Abdel-Rahman,** the blind advocate of the use of force against all **"infidels,"** who died in an American prison on February 18, 2017. In angry harangues issuing from his refuge in the US since 1990, he denounced Egypt's secularist leaders as corrupt pharaohs and infidels. While clothing himself in Muslim religious garb, and holding himself out as **"a learned Muslim Sheikh,"** he proclaimed that **"faithful Muslims had a duty to wage jihad … to install a government in Egypt that would obey the strictest Islamic laws."**[34]

Abdel-Rahman (a name whose translation from Arabic is **"The Servant of God the Merciful"**) was completely off the mark on Islamic law in more than one count. He arrogated for himself the power of the Creator who alone is the judge of fidelity, and only on Judgement Day. There is no jihad in the use of force beyond repelling an aggression coming from beyond the national border. Abdel-Rahman also abused the locus of his foreign refuge, America, whose laws should have been observed in regard to the prevention of the advocacy of the use of force internally or externally.

It was therefore not surprising that **deposed Egyptian President Morsi**

---

[33] *""*

[34] The New York Times, February 19, 2017, p.22.

had, during the Islamist reign in Egypt (2012-2013) made his calls on the US to release Abdel-Rahman from imprisonment a foreign policy priority. That demand was duly rebuffed.

In his speech before the German Bundestag, the Grand Imam of Al-Azhar said in Arabic: **"Islam does not permit the killing of non-Muslims because of their non-adherence of Islam or of any other religion. For God has created both believers and non-believers."** From the perspective of jihadism, apostasy is the stigma of Muslims who, for one reason or another, have left Islam or a precept thereof for whatever reason.

The quote from Dr. El-Taiyeb's Berlin statement has the Quran's full backing where it says: **"God is the One who created you, and, of you, there are some who are unbelievers and some are believers, and God sees all that you do." (Chapter 64/Verse 2)**

Judging by the Quran, the principal pillar of Islamic faith, one should wonder as to the source of, for example, the draconian Pakistani laws which match in their severity those of Saudi Arabia, regarding apostasy. From media reports, one learns that it is enough for a disgruntled neighbor to accuse another of apostasy to have them subjected to torture and even death.

While a death industry has arisen out of takfirism in the East, in the West an industry of the search for financial rewards and stardom has taken root. The prime example of that are publicists like **Ayaan Hirsi Ali.** In her, we have a Somali who has been lionized in the West due to her renunciation of both nationality and the faith in which she was born. Her books, **"Heretic"** and **"Infidel,"** provide probative evidence. Quoting from the back cover of **Infidel**, we read the following: **"Infidel shows the coming of age of this distinguished political superstar and champion of free speech as well as the development of her beliefs, iron will, and extraordinary determination to fight injustice."**[35]

Yet describing tribal experiences in Somalia, clothed in the garb of Islam, is far removed from the facts of Islam and its law and practices. And objectively, one should wonder: Are Hirsi's diatribes against the faith of 1.7 billion Muslims an objective exercise of free speech? It looks like Hirsi's advocacy for **"the reform of Islam"** is a confirmation of the jihadi takfiris belief that Islam is under attack world-wide -a justification for their world-

---

[35] Aayan Hirsi Ali, (New York: Free Press, 2007).

wide criminality.

While the power of an individual to declare another an apostate, though religiously and morally baseless, Islamic Law itself would deny the infliction of punishment for such bogus claim. The Prophet Muhammad had regarded all human beings as a fraternity. He had declared: **"O God: I profess that I am your subject and messenger. O my God and the God of everything, I profess that all human beings are a fraternity."**

As stated above, this Muhammadan tradition has its roots in the Quran. It sets forth this cardinal principle of freedom of thought. Flowing from this basis is the dire consequence of ignoring it. Again to the above-cited speech by Dr. El-Taiyeb to the Myanmar youth in Cairo, where he said: **"Exclusion and marginalization always lead to shedding of blood and displacement of the innocent."**[36]

In his book, on **Salafi-Jihadism, Shiraz Maher** deals with takfir under the title of **"establishing disbelief."** Tracing its rise to the 2003 invasion of Iraq, he rightly attributes it to the erroneous construction by those terrorists of the Islamic rules of war. Referring to the the then leader of Al-Qaeda in Iraq, **Musab al-Zarqawi,** Maher says that al-Zarqawi, during his lifetime **"employed it liberally to license a fratricidal civil war against the Iraqi Shia community."**[37]

Then he goes on to say that takfir **"for the global jihad movement … has become a valuable tool for expelling those from the faith who are thought to be subverting it from within."**[38]

Takfirism is, therefore, thought by takfiris to be the equivalent of a nuclear option, especially as it makes its victim an enemy of God. The Quran says: **"Whoever is an enemy to God and His Angels and messengers, to Gabriel and Michael, -lo! God is an enemy to those who reject faith."**[39] In Islamic Law, **"faith"** is whatever a faithful person believes in. It

---

[36] Dr. El-Taiyeb, Speech at the dialogue held in Cairo on Myanmar, December 2016.

[37] Shiraz Maher, Salafi-Jihadism: The History of an Idea (New York: Oxford University Press, 2016), p.71.

[38] Id.

[39] The Quran, Chapter 2, Verse 98.

is an inclusive definition, with no particularization, as could seen in the various utterances of Sheikh Al-Azhar.

Islamic Law places an overwhelming emphasis on avoidance of **Fitna (insurrection),** even if the ruler is unjust. But under takfirism, Muslim against Muslim became an accepted norm. This can be seen in the first armed confrontation in Basra, Iraq in 656 AD (the Battle of Camel). **It pitted Ali, the fourth and last "enlightened Califa,"** against the forces opposing him. Those were led by Aisha, the young widow of the Prophet Muhammad and her cohorts. Ali won, but the cleavage in Muslim society remained dangerously deep until today. This has been a historic result of takfirism, even prior to the age of jihadism.

From the foregoing it becomes clear that Takfirism was born at the dawn of Islam. But jihadism, the apt name for today's terrorism, found in it a useful blunt instrument to cow down their opponents. For that reason, **Dr. El-Taiyeb, in his speech in Russia,** delivered on August 25, 2016 lumped together takfirism, sectarian violence, and the inter-Muslim Mazhab (School) quarrels, as leading to the same result -the demeaning of the name of Islam.

The easy access to social media has enabled Salafi-jihadism to extend its reach. It is said that twitter has made it possible for Salafis in Saudi Arabia to reach 14 million adherents.[40]

Those included Salafis in Egypt who have **consistently engaged in takfiring Shiism in Egypt.** That medium has enabled Saudi Arabia, in her strategic conflict with Iran for hegemony in the Gulf, to translate it into a Sunni-Shii religious confrontation. That metamorphosis from political to religious became more acute following the entry into the Syrian civil war of Iran's Revolutionary Guards and Lebanon's Hezbollah.

With stability being the cornerstone in Islam for a governable community, takfir has emerged as a destabilizer. Among other things, it legitimates intra-Muslim violence. Rebellions and other forms of dissent have generally not been tolerated, even if the purpose was the removal of an unjust ruler. This premise has been manipulated by the Muslim Brotherhood in Egypt prior to the success of the **revolution of January 25. 2011.** Though the Brotherhood changed its position later by joining the ranks of that

---

[40] Al-Quds Al-Arabi, London and New York, February 22, 2017, p.5 (translated from Arabic).

revolution, its leaders had earlier called the effort to remove Mubarak unislamic.

The Prophet Muhammad had been authentically quoted as saying: **"If a person says to his brother, oh unbeliever! Then surely one of them is such."**[41] The symbiotic link between takfir and jihadism solidified after the invasion of Iraq in 2003. Following the start of that war of choice, Paul Bremer, the proconsul of the US invaders, foolishly disbanded the huge Iraqi army. Maher stresses this point as he says in his book referenced above: **"This was when al-Qaeda and its supporters from the broader ecosystem of Salafi-Jihadi thinking were forced to produce a dense and detailed body of work explaining the jurisprudential framework behind their understanding of takfir."**[42]

Even by during early Wahhabism, **Ibn Abdel al-Wahhab** its reformist founder, takfirism leading to jihadism was unrecognizable. That is because that founder had **"remained faithful to his vision of reforming Islamic beliefs and practices through education. He did not set up a jihadi-oriented community bent on military conquest or a terrorist training camp providing specialized classes in the use of weapons, bomb construction, or the planning of suicide missions."**[43]

The Quran forcefully rebuts the claim by the takfiris to the power of declaring who is faithful to Islam and who is not. It instructs Muhammad to stand firm in declaring that in matters of faith, God is the decider. **"The command rests with none but God. He decrees the Truth, and He is the Best of Judges."**[44] In Quranic Arabic, the term **"Best of Judges"** is incisive. It means that God, the Just, though His Wisdom separates between truth and falsehood.

The Quran also calls on Muhammad to declare: **"Say, 'O people, surely there has come to you the Truth from your Lord, whoever is guided, is guided only for his own soul, and whoever goes astray, he is astray**

---

[41] Maher, Op. Cit., p. 75, quoting from Al-Bukhari, Vol. 8, Book 73.

[42] Natana J. Delong-Bas, Wahhabi Islam, Op.Cit., p. 38.

[43] Ibid.

[44] The Quran, Chapter 6, Verse 57.

only for his own soul, and I am not a trustee over you."[45]

That is the heart of freedom of thought in Islam -the title of an entire book by the late **Gamal El-Banna.** An Islamic expression of what we, in international law, call **"the right to self-determination"** for both the individual and the nation.

So who are those misfits to excommunicate any body for any faith? Furthermore, the term **"excommunicate"** itself is not known in the Muslim faith. A long beard, and a loose garment, and an embroidered turban do not bestow on those sporting them any extra-terrestrial authority to drum someone out of their faith.

The most grievous aggression by the takfiris is directed toward the Shia. In my research on Sunnism and Shiism, I am finding that that split is a historical hoax for the lack of any authentic religious evidence. Takfirism has thrived on the back of that hoax. Maher in his book rightly maintains that: **"They (the Sunnis) … deride the Shia for their hostility towards the Sahaba (the Prophet's companion), the community whom the contemporary Salafi movement aims to emulate."[46]**

The centrality of the issue of takfirism is that it plays a primordial role in jihadism. In essence, it is one of the several frameworks within which jihadism administers its poison. It arrogates for its practitioners dual roles: **One that belongs to the Creator (God is the Judge), and one that belongs to every individual (the right to personal choice).**

---

[45] ________________, Chapter 10, Verse 108.

[46] Maher, op. cit.

CHAPTER 6

The Abuse of the **"Fatwa"**

Since 1998, the massive abuse of the Fatwa has been a jihadi weapon. The date is stated here to signify the first time that Osama Bin Laden had taken to issuance of fatwas. By doing so, he was deliberately using that tool for both self-legitimation and recruitment for his criminal cause.

Fatwa is generally defined as a legal opinion or decree handed down by an Islamic religious leader. In Arabic dictionaries, the definition is much closer to what it actually is - **"a response"** (i.e. an advisory opinion) in regard to an issue or a problem on which there is no text in the Quran, or guidance in Muhammad's traditions (the Sunna). The authority issuing a fatwa is invariably highlighted. For example, the Grand Imam of Al-Azhar, has been the issuing source, until a special department, called **"The House of the Fatwa,"** was established.

From the above, it could be discerned that Bin Laden and his murderous successors were clothed with no authority to issue fatwas. They simply lacked the scholarship required to enable them to guide anyone to the correct Islamic answer to any problem in these changing times.

What compounds the dilemma of jihadis issuing fatwas, is that whereas such advisory opinions have no uniform mechanisms for enforcement, the jihadis arrogated for themselves enforcement means, most of which were capital punishment.

In essence, the role of the fatwa, though as an unenforced counsel, has a substantial persuasive edge. That is particularly so for an illiterate public. This aspect of influence through fatwa is made abundantly clear in the

Quran.

The following quotations are a selection. In the first of these, God addresses the Prophet Muhammad in these words: **"(If) They consult you, say: 'God instructs you concerning those who leave no descendants...'"** (Chapter 4/Verse 176). Reference is made here to the question of inheritance. In another chapter (sura), the Quran says, again in the form of God addressing His messenger: **"Do not enter, therefore, into controversies concerning them, except on a matter that is clear, nor consult any of them about..."** (Chapter 18/Verse 23).

Casting the fatwa in the framework of an optional guiding compass does not derogate from its impact as a interpretation by a qualified scholar of Islam of a matter of either faith or life mode. We here note that the several volumes of fatwas rendered by Ibn Taimiyah, a conservative Islamic scholar (died in the 14th century AD), have continued till today, to guide strict thought. It represents a hodgepodge of opinions thrown together as a soup alphabet of principles. From contracts to alcohol, and from virtue to entertainment. All put in a straight jacket.

Strict orientation through fatwas was possible because Islam, in its openness to a variety of interpretations, has induced a broad variety of opinions. It created a constant dependency by the public on others for guidance. Examples of Ibn Taimiyah's avalanche of fatwas can be endless. Among these are his rules on playing chess (fatwa #1022). He posited the question: **"Is playing chess sinful, avoidable or permissible?"** On this, he cited the view of a Moroccan scholar (Abu-Omar Ibn Abdel-Burr) who disallowed chess playing if it caused a delay in the performance of one of the 5 daily prayers on time. [47]

Such a stretch of reasoning defies two well-known elements in Islamic jurisprudence: that religion is **"ease not a burden,"** and that the Quran does not even mention how many daily prayers are to be performed. The 5 daily prayers are a tradition of the Prophet Muhammad who had also said on the matter of prayers **"take your ease"** (La Haraj).

The **Grand Fawas** of Ibn Taimiyah, with a view to making chess playing by Muslims a potential sin, then delve into the Quran in search of tortured evidence. His reasoning goes from disallowing that sport, which began as a

---

[47] Ibn Taimiyah, <u>The Great Fatwas</u>, Vol. 4 (Beirut, Dar Al-Kotob Al-ilmiyah, 2002) pp. 455-456.

Persian tradition, to citation of the Quran. **"Woe to those who pray; but are heedless of their prayers."** [48] Here is Ibn Taimiyah's interpretation: a totally failing deduction, citing an explanation of this Quranic chapter through an earlier fatwa-maker (Salman Al-Farisi). He quotes the latter's opining that **"Delay in praying on time is a nullification of its effects in terms of God's rewards."** [49]

Thus life of a Muslim, in the eyes of the likes of Ibn Taimiyah, is unfortunately bracketed through fatwas between bookends: heaven and hell. This is the antithesis of the new religious Islamic revolution.

At this juncture of exposing the abuse of the Fatwa by jihadis and their non-jihadi enablers, we turn to Sheikh El-Taiyeb of Al-Azhar. His speech on May 2016 at Abuja, Nigeria devoted 10% of its content to this very issue. In the presence of Nigeria's President Muhammad Buhari, the Grand Imam of Al-Azhar pointed out the confrontation by the new Islamic revolution against jihadism on the battlefront of the fatwas in 3 ways:[50]

He implored Islamic scholars to **"face the realities of today through containing the crisis of fatwas in Islam."** Then added: **"They have to shoulder their responsibilities towards clarifying the truth of this faith which centers on Islam's clear call for brotherhood, connectedness and peace amongst people east and west."** Here we should recall that the Grand Imam of Al-Azhar was uttering these historic Islamic principles in the land where Boko Haram has been delegitimating western learning.

On a secondary level, El-Taiyeb was recalling **"the jurisdiction of good diversity (differentiation)."** Here are his words on this point translated by me from the original Arabic: **"I mean the value of diversity which has always been one of the main ingredients of enriching the renaissance of the Muslim Ummah."**

From there, he deduced a third level of argumentation against the abuse of the Fatwa which led to jihadi mayhem and criminality throughout the world. Thus he advocated: **"leaving people with what they have been culturally brought up to coalesce around -their ijmaa (unanimity on a**

---

[48] The Quran, Chapter 107, verses 4 and 5.

[49] Ibn Taimiyah, op. Cit., p. 456

[50] El-Taiyeb, Statement at Abuja, Nigeria, May 2016.

geographic basis)." Detailing that point, Sheikh El-Taiyeb posited that: **"Whatever this Muslim nation (ummah) has agreed upon should be the standard of differentiation between what is right and what is wrong. Let us not decide for people the legitimacy of only one Mazhab (school of thought) in faith, worship... Let us teach our children that the good salaf (forebears), starting from the Sahabas (the Companions of the Prophet Muhammad) throughout their golden years, had differed amongst themselves. But without animus leading to separation from one another.**

Concluding this important advocacy for sanity and authenticity in issuing fatwas by those who are so qualified, the Grand Imam of Al-Azhar warned in Abuja against **"uncontrollable differences which have inculcated in some Muslims the urge to excommunicating others and perpetrating violence against them as profligates. This situation has enabled certain forces to play mischievously with the unity of the Ummah."**

By far, one of the most notorious fatwas is the takfir of the Shias. It has weaponized the fiction of having a Sunni Islam and a Shii Islam. This has resulted in a historic rupture in the body of the Ummah with dire consequences, especially in the Gulf area. Amazingly, the entire Sunni-Shii dichotomy has occurred in the 7th century AD as a result of a political choice of Muhammad's successors. Imam Ali, the Prophet's cousin and son in law was passed over three times for that central post. In my research, I found no religious basis for that split. The only dispute was politically-based, not religiously anchored.

Throughout the ages, the Islamic adage has been: **"there is no difference between an Arab and a non-Arab (Ajami -meaning non-Arab) except on the basis of piety."** What compounds the error of that myth of Sunni vs. Shii, are irresponsible fatwas. The Quran's basic outlook is that humanity is one. This principle was driven home by the Grand Imam of Al-Azhar, especially in his Abuja, Nigeria, speech.

With reference to the role and quality of the fatwa, as a faith-enhancer, Dr. El-Taiyeb was professional in his speech in Paris in 2016. This was in the context of his advocacy for transitioning from **"the jurisprudence of minorities"** (the Shias are 10% of the entire Muslim population of 1.7 billions), to **"the jurisdiction of positive fusion and co-existence."** Moving beyond that foundational premise, the Sheikh of Al-Azhar said: **"Our jurisprudential rules establish that the fatwas change with the**

changing of time, place, circumstances, and persons issuing them."[51]

Against this background, one may discern the idiocy of individuals like Osama Bin Laden, or Abu-Musab Al-Zarqawi, or Al-Baghdadi of ISIS, terrorists all, manufacturing fatwas for advocacy and recruitment. THe same delegitimation of such false fatwas is applicable to a Saudi judge by the name of Moaz Bin Abdel-Aziz Al-Mubarad, the author of a recent book entitled: **"Law Schools and Un-Islamic Rule."**

That book is premised on a frontal attack on the curricula of law schools in Saudi Arabia, especially the university of King Saud in Riyadh. The author's thesis, which was endorsed by two members of **"the Permanent Fatwas Committee,"** and of **"two Grand Islamic Scholars, Sheikh Al-Fawzan and Sheikh Al-Barak. Their endorsement was to the effect that those law schools advocate apostasy through their teaching of secular laws."**

Vilifying all legal education in law schools throughout the entire Muslim world, the book's author, as supported by the Saudi Permanent Fatwas Committee, advances the following fallacies: glorification of secular laws negates God's Sharia laws; an enhancement of adultery, intoxication, usury and forbidden carnal behavior; and denigrating Islamic jurisprudence as being capable of meeting the demands of the present age. All lunacies!!

The Wahhabi ideology of the book, issued as a fatwas compendium worthy of the Ibn Taiimia's so-called **"Grand Fatwas,"** directs its biggest guns to contract law. To the author and his endorsers who constitute the corpus of the Saudi Permanent Fatwas Committee rely on an earlier false fatwa by Saudi Sheikh Abdulla Al-Mahmoud to the effect that a contract, formed on the basis of an offer and acceptance, is **"nothing but subterfuge."**

The upshot of that publication is a mandatory call for **"jihad against those propagators of secular legal education."** Fighting those perpetrators, the author advocates, should be waged **"until they repent, and accept the rules of the sanctifying sharia."**[52] Is it any wonder that, on those faulty bases, the West regards Islam as **"a cult?"**

---

[51] El-Taiyeb, Statement in Paris, France, June 2016.

[52] As reported by the daily newspaper, Al-Quds Al-Arabi (London and New York: March 31, 2016)

As an enhancer of jihadi ideology, the abuse of the fatwa is but one demonstration of the timelines of the new Islamic religious revolution. This is especially salutary as that ideological reset brings to mind fully **"the jurisdiction of filling the textual gaps"** in both the Quran and the Muhamadan tradition (the Sunna).

As stated above, the process of gaps filling, known as ijtihad (the application of thought, known as wisdom to the text) has been urged by both the Quran and the Prophet Muhammad. The Quran states: **"Our Lord send to them a Messenger from them who shall recite your Revelations to them and teach them the Book (Quran) and the Wisdom and purify them…"[53]**

It was only through ijtihad that sharia was able to adapt through the ages, thus becoming **"relevant to all times and places."** Unanimity among local Islamic scholars issuing a fatwa has been praised by Muhammad who said: **"My Ummah cannot be collectively wrong on a matter reached through unanimity."**

Denying the legitimacy of secular legislation, which in any case has always avoided negating sharia, as wrongly posited by the above-cited Saudi book, is also a violation of what can be clearly extrapolated from the Quran. It urges respect for **"God and obey the Messenger (meaning Muhammad), and those entrusted with authority over you."[54]** Legislators fall in the category of persons entrusted with authority (in Arabic, Ulu Al-Amr).

In a later chapter in this book on ijtihad, the example of Muhammad's welcoming of the application of common sense in the formulation of judgments in matters where neither the Quran nor the Sunna have supplied a clear text. That citation is on point in regard to a judge's ruling -the subject matter of legal education which Wahhabism is ignorantly denying.

A professor of law at Harvard, Noah Feldman, dealt with this issue of supplementing Sharia by learned interpretation. In an article entitled: **"What Sharia Is and Isn't,"** he advances the following: **"Fiqh refers to the interpretation and application of Shariah in the real world. Fiqh is Islamic law as practiced by people."**

---

[53] <u>The Quran</u>, Chapter 2, Verse 129.

[54] <u>Ibid.</u>, Chapter 4, Verse 59.

Then Feldman refers to the situation in Saudi Arabia, saying: **"In Saudi Arabia where there is no written constitution, classical Islamic legal principles function as a kind of unwritten common-law constitution. But even Saudi Arabia has a body of administrative regulations that function a lot like legislation."**[55] That opinion advanced by professor Feldman was in response to Newt Gingrich's a faulty proposal for a religious inquisition of Muslims advanced by Newt Gingrich, a former Republican Speaker of America's House of Representative.

Attacking that proposal, Noah Feldman opened up his article by: **"Fortunately, no one is going to follow Newt Gingrich's unconstitutional and un-American plan for an inquisition to 'test every person here who is a Muslim' and deport the ones who believe in Sharia."**

Unfortunately, the Feldman's prediction of non-pursuit of the Gingrich proposal which was issued in the heat of the aftermath of the terrorist attack in Nice, France, through murder by truck, was hollowed by Donald Trump. The 45th President of the U.S. issued not one but two executive orders reflecting his campaign's calls for **"extreme vetting"** of Muslims entering the U.S. Though the enforcement of those presidential orders was stayed by federal judicial rulings, the episodes reflected the danger of misunderstanding of Islamic law as being what the jihadis say it is.

The adverse effects on global security of those misunderstandings of Islamic law by both the West and the East cannot be underestimated. The jihadist ideology has permeated the global outlook on Islam to the point of converting Islamophobia into what amounts now to **"War on Islam"** itself. In his speech in Paris in May 2016, Sheikh El-Taiyeb, a graduate of the Sorbonne, bemoaned the French tragedy resulting from jihadism, in the following words: **"Beautiful Paris witnessed a dark night resulting from the death of about 140 innocent victims... a dark terrorism which is repugnant to both East and West."**[56]

---

[55] Noah Feldman, "What Shariah Is (and Isn't)," <u>The New York Times</u>, Sunday, July 17, 2016, p.3.

[56] El-Taiyeb's speech in Paris, May 2016.

CHAPTER 7

Insurrection As a Global Tool of Jihadism (FITNAH)

Jihadism, interpreted as **"insurrection,"** is regarded by Islamic Law as the worst calamity that can befall a community. In Arabic **"Fitnah,"** it is mentioned in the Quran more than 30 times. Referring to **"Fitnah"** as **"tumult,"** the Quran says: **"tumult and oppression are worse than slaughter."**[57] With jihadism looking upon tumult as a means for the establishment of an **"Islamic State"** (alternatively called a Caliphate as in the case of ISIS), Al-Azhar totally disagrees with this reasoning.

In the aftermath of the Egyptian revolution of January 2011, Al-Azhar issued a document in August of that year, billed by Dr. Ahmed El-Taiyeb **"Al-Azhar Document on Egypt's Future."**[58] It was billed as **"the product of a unique consensus among leaders in various fields of faith, politics, laws, art, literature, history, society, psychology, and other areas of academia."**

That historic document consisted of eleven principles, presaging the new Islamic religious revolution which was launched by Al-Azhar in 2014 at the start of the presidency of Egypt by Abdel-Fattah El-Sisi. The first of these principles, which guided the drafting of the 2014 Secular Constitution, stated: **"Islam, in its legislation, civilization, and history does not recognize a 'religiously-based' State."**

---

[57] The Quran, Chapter 2, Verse 191.

[58] Al-Azhar Document of Eleven Principles, "Document on Egypt's Future," August 20, 2011.

The denial by Al-Azhar in August 2011 of the legitimacy of any Islamic State led later to the attempts by the regime of the Muslim Brotherhood (June 2012-June 2013) to the downgrading of Al-Azhar. These attempts failed miserably. Here it should be recognized that the popular recall of the presidency of Mohamed Morsi in early July 2013, backed by Egypt's armed forces led by El-Sisi, saved Egypt from civil war between the Islamists, later turned jihadists, and the majority of the Egyptian populace.

Averting the threat of civil war in the most populous Arab country, was, in effect, a guarantee of the continuity of the historic look by the Egyptians, whether civil or military, upon their country as a secular State. During the interregnum in the presidency of Egypt, from the fall of Mubarak to the rise of Morsi to that presidency (February 2011-June 2012), Egypt was governed by the Egyptian Supreme Council of the Armed Forces (SCAF). Stressing the secularity of Egypt, as a historic antidote against **"fitnah,"** the SCAF Deputy Chairman, General Sami Anan stated: **"The Secularity of the State is a matter of national security which is not negotiable."**[59]

As tumult, or insurrection, must per force resort to arms, the denial of its legitimacy as a form of jihadism was reflected in Dr. El-Taiyeb's speech before the Bundestag in Berlin on March 15, 2016. These were his words: **"It is not true what is said about Islam being a religion of combat and a faith based on the sword. The word 'sword' is not part of the vocabulary of the Quran. Not once was it mentioned in the Book."** [60]

In the same speech, the Grand Imam of Al-Azhar posed to his European audience this rhetorical question: **"You may ask: 'If Islam and Muslims reflect this rosy image, then how have those armed Islamic movements, like ISIS (Daesh) and its affiliates, get out of this Islamic garb? My response is that if every faith were to be judged by the criminal actions perpetrated by some of its adherents, then no faith shall be immune from the charge of violence and terrorism."**[61]

A prime demonstration of jihadi fomenting of insurrection (fitna) is the

---

[59] As reported by this author in conjunction with his reporting on Al-Azhar's document of August 2011.

[60] El-Taiyeb's speech before the Bundestag, March 15, 2016.

[61] Ibid.

attack perpetrated by ISIS on the Coptic churches in Egypt (Tanta and Alexandria) on Palm Sunday, April 9, 2017. Gloating at the carnage, which killed more than 40 innocent persons among worshippers and security personnel, DAESH claimed victory over the El-Sisi government. A hollow claim demonstrating the depravity of that crime, the vacuousness of that so-called victory, and the resilience of anti-jihadism reflected in the declaration of a state of emergency for 3 months.

Unfortunately, such criminal activities are nearly impossible to eliminate completely. No organized State could muster the muscle and the intelligence-gathering to ward off the evil represented by an individual determined to kill himself and harm others as well. It was an overplay of adjectives used by the **New York Times** as it referred to those events as **"Attacks Show(ing) ISIS' strategy for Egypt: Gaining Ground by Killing Christians."**[62] Such screaming headlines in major media outlets are nothing short of indirectly buying into the dangerous jihadi narrative.

By comparison, the authentic voice of the new Islamic religious revolution is ironically muted. In Abuja, the Grand Imam of Al-Azhar raised that voice: **"The scourge of terrorism, this grand calamity and poisonous plant, has begun to produce its bitter harvest. Hatred of Islam and the Muslims have spread among the adherents of other religions. That is particularly so in the West where it has become confusing to discern right from wrong in Islam."**[63]

It was a call repeated from an earlier address by Dr. El-Taiyeb in Berlin where he had unequivocally condemned **"the blind insurrection which legitimates the shedding of blood and the destruction of homelands."** From that point, he went on to demonstrate some of the various means for combating jihadism, **"including roving missions (caravans) which traverse the world calling for universal peace and the protection of youth from descent into the precipice of terrorism."**[64]

Referring specifically to Christians and the adherents of other faiths, the Sheikh of Al-Azhar called it **"a heinous crime"** to **"attack them in the name of religion as this is a rebellion against Islam."** His call was for

---

[62] The New York Times, April 11, 2017, p.A6.

[63] Dr. El-Taiyeb, Abuja speech, May 2016.

[64] _______, Berlin speech, op. cit.

Christians and other non-Muslims to stay put in their homelands until the wave of terrorism which afflicts us all at present is no more.[65]

It was not therefore surprising that the ISIS attacks through suicide bombing at the Coptic churches in Tanta and Alexandria in April 2017 were the object of condemnation by official and non-governmental Egypt. One such non-governmental organization was The Egyptian Organization for the Protection of the Constitution. In its statement of April 10, 2017; it said: **"the greatest threat which challenges Egyptian society at present is terrorism. The successive terrorist crimes which have targeted Christian citizens at the Cathedral (Dec. 2016), northern Sinai, and lately at Tanta and Alexandria have one objective: the sowing of the seeds of sectarian insurrection and the destruction of the principle of citizenship enshrined in the Constitution."**

From condemnation, that non-governmental organization went on to call for swift measures to confront that insurrection, including: **"the establishment of a national commission against discrimination which is called for by Article 53 of the Egyptian Constitution (2014)."** Those proposals also included **"the institution of a comprehensive strategy against terrorism. Such strategy would not be confined to security measures only. It should also cover institutional reform of education, culture, religious education, and religious institutions."**[66]

Looking at **"insurrection"** from a global perspective, one should include the enablers of jihadism through their frontal attacks on Muslim immigrants. It is true that some of those displaced persons have angered their host countries through non-integration. But the narrative spun out by anti-Muslim advocates has crossed the line to the point of blaming those isolated incidents on the faith itself. A neighbor of Mr. Trump, George Guido Lombardi, a point man for Europe's populism, has sounded a false alarm. Lombardi is reported to envision Putin **"as the champion of the spiritual descendants of World War II resistance fighters."**[67]

Pouring more gasoline on the fire of anti-Islamism, Lombardi praised the

---

[65] Ibid.

[66] The Egyptian Organization for the Protection of the Constitution, statement of April 10, 2017, regarding terrorism on Palm Sunday, Friday, April 17, 2017.

[67] The New York Times, April 15, 2017, p.A5.

European leaders of the extreme right. He said: **"Le Pen, Geert…all the resistance is fighting the Nazi Islamists."**[68] This is while the Grand Imam of Al-Azhar, in his Paris speech of June 2016 addressed the negative effects of non-integration of Muslims in the West. Said he: **"Among the problems (of inter-faith amity) are the calls by these Muslims for keeping their distance psychologically from European society… And on the European side, there are the negative information material which hurt Muslims and depict them to the European street in an unfair manner."**[69]

In Islamic law, FITNAH (insurrection) is assessed as a total disaster not only because of the disappearance of law and order. But also because it triggers a trauma buried deeply in the Arab psyche. It is the trauma of tribal warfare which was common in Arabia before the faith of Islam was born. Looking at the map of the Arabian peninsula, one sees through pre-Islamic eyes a huge nearly rectangular barren land. Encapsulated between the Gulf to the east, the Indian Ocean to the south, the Red Sea to the west, and **"the Syrian desert"** to the north.

That was not only physical barrenness. It was also, 1400 years ago, cultural barrenness compared to the great civilizations besieging it. These were the Persian to the east, the Mesopotamia to the north-east, the byzantine to the north, and the Egyptian to the west of the Red Sea. Just look hard!! Do you see any monuments to speak of at that pre-Islamic epoch except for the Kaabah, a house of adoration considered to be that of Abraham and his son Ismail? The only civilized portion was Yemen (Arabia Felix). Of course there was poetry, and love of wine, and trade movements by huge caravans, with the tribe of Quraish based in Mecca, enriching Quraish, the home town of the Prophet Muhammad who also had partaken of trade himself. (Quraish means the moneyed tribe, from the word Qirsh, a monetary unit).

Thus Islam came to Arabia not only as a monotheistic faith, but also as a civilizing mission. It liberated women from being mere chattel, to gender equality; elevated the dignity of the poor; equalized between the faiths within and outside of the Arabian enclosure. It was a revolution which insisted on ending tribal warfare. Regression from that new status was insurrection, the most feared calamity in a basically tribal setting. And the tribe was, and largely continues to be, the most comfortable of all zones for

---

[68] <u>Id</u>.

[69] El-Taiyeb, speech in Paris, June 2016.

the citizen.[70]

Jihadism has therefore to be understood in the context of an insurrection, now with a global projection. This represents a total decline from the great ethos of tolerance towards **"the other"** in regard to diversity of faith. Ahmed Amin, quoted above, in turn quotes from German sources as he writes: **"What differentiates the Islamic realm from Christian Europe of the middle ages is this: In the former resides a great number of adherents of religions beside Islam. But not in the latter."**

Then he goes on to a more focused explanation: It was by necessity that Jews and Muslims have lived with the Muslims side by side. This coexistence produced an environment of tolerance not known in Europe of the middle ages."[71]

What a far cry is this from the letter addressed by Osama Bin Laden to the American people rationalizing the 9/11 attacks. In it the now dead leader of Al-Qaeda says: **"Al-Qaeda attacked the US"** because **"you attacked us and continue to attack us."** Then he proceeded to expose his confused thinking as he states: **"Under your supervision, consent and orders, the governments of our countries, which act as your agents, attack us on a daily basis; these governments prevent our people from establishing the Islamic sharia, using violence and lies to do so."**[72]

In these wild utterances, there are layers upon layers of insurrection messages: First: Who gave Bin Laden the authority to speak in the name of all Muslims; second: Islamic law does not establish a State; it sets up a community; third: Those 3000 innocent persons who perished in those criminal attacks, including a large number of Muslims, had nothing to do with foreign policy decisions affecting Arab or Muslim lands. In Islamic law, each of those who perished on 9/11 is regarded as **"martyrs"** (shaheed).

It was therefore incumbent upon the Grand Imam of Al-Azhar to declare

---

[70] Ahmed Amin, <u>The Dawn of Islam</u> (Beirut: Dar Al-Kotob Al-Ilmiyah, 2009), 3rd edition, pp.22-23 (on Arab Social Life).

[71] ______, <u>Mid-Morning of Islam</u> (Cairo, Maktabat Al-Nahda Al-Misriyah, 1961), Vol. One, p.322.

[72] As quoted by Shiraz Maher, <u>op</u>. <u>cit</u>., p.45

in his keynote address at Al-Azhar's symposium in Cairo on **"Confronting Extremism and Terrorism"** in 2014 the following: **"These heinous and barbaric crimes clothed themselves in the garb of Islam, this faith of piety. Their perpetrators launched from their dens from which they plan their crimes, the name of "The Islamic State" or "The State of the Islamic Caliphate."** Such names and cliches are nothing but an attempt to export the image of a new fake Islam. They regard their Islam as a religion which justifies butchery and beheadings of anyone who oppose it.[73] An authoritative appeal from **"insurrection"** which constitutes corrective principle of the on-going new Islamic religious revolution, voiced by the leader of the venerable Al-Azhar.

Such a call has other ideological objectives. These are: defeating the concept of resurrecting a caliphate in any form; the other is to legitimize **"insurrection"** against an unjust ruler.

In regard to the caliphate,[74] the hideous urgings by the ISIS leader, Abu-Bakr Al-Baghdadi, flies in the face of history. The reign of the Caliphates ended with the assassination of Imam Ali, Muhammad's cousin and son-in-law (January, 27, 661 AD). Successive presumptive caliphates were just that -presumptive. That is not to mention the established fact that Al-Baghdadi is a mere Iraqi thug from Anbar.

Analyzing the other objective, namely justifying insurrection, Al-Azhar's basic documents published in Arabic in Cairo in 2012, provide the following reasoning in support of the popular will. Those papers stressed that: **"The ruler who sheds the blood of his people loses his legitimacy. This is provided that such insurrection is a peaceful mass uprising, representing the people's aspirations, not the greed of the forces lying in wait to pounce upon the Arabs and Muslims."[75]**

Such forceful criminalization by Al-Azhar applies, among other things, to Bashar Al-Assad of Syria, Since 2011, that war criminal has caused the

---

[73] Dr. El-Taiyeb, Keynote address at Al-Azhar's Symposium on Extremism and Terrorism, Cairo, Hotel Marriot, December 3, 2014.

[74] Hugh Kennedy, <u>Caliphate From Grand to Sordid</u> (Basic Books), as reviewed in the <u>New York Review of Books</u>, January 29, 2017.

[75] Al-Azhar Al-Sharif Documents, 2012, including Al-Azhar's declaration of December 30, 2011.

death of half a million of his subjects in a hopeless attempt to remain the president of a flattened Syria. Fighting injustice is a basic concept of Islamic law which is also enshrined in international law, applicable to self-defense and international humanitarian intervention.

Herein lies the heart of the struggle between good and evil, glorified in the Quran in this verse: **"Thus doth God (by parables) show forth truth and vanity. For the scum disappears like froth cast out; while that which is for the good of mankind remains on the earth."**[76]

It is of historic interest to find that the purchase of a copy of the Quran by Thomas Jefferson **"helped (to) develop an attitude of religious tolerance."**[77] That assessment of the views of the third president of the US came to us through Swineheart's review of a book by Denise A. Spellberg, titled: **Thomas Jefferson's Quran: Islam and the Founders.**

Amazingly, the Quran, in the hands of an American President and a confirmed world statesman, can inspire tolerance, while in the hands of a bandit like Al-Baghdadi and his ilk can lead to committing genocide and the prolongation of this global insurrection called jihadism.

---

[76] The Quran, Chapter 13, Verse 17.

[77] Kirk Davis Swineheart, "People of the Book" in The New York Review of Books, November 17, 2013, p.17

CHAPTER 8

Diversity Is Central to Universality

In the introduction to his book, **Diversity in Muslim Society,** Gamal El-Banna, says: **"Some people have wrongly thought the following: Since Islam is a faith which advocates monotheism (God Is One), known as Tawheed, therefore everything in society should be uniform. The error here is that such advocacy puts Muslim society in one non-changeable, non-evolving form lacking diversity."[78]**

We see the same emphasis on diversity, which is now propelling the new Islamic Religious Revolution in Al-Azhar's declaration of August 17, 2011. It was issued within only 7 months following what that document called **"the turbulence of the Revolution of January 25, 1011 which swept aside the military rule of 60 years."[79]**

The second principle of this eleven-principles historic document states as follows: **"Democratic rule is based on free and direct elections which encapsulate the modern formulation of the application of the Islamic precepts of Shura (consultation). Such rule guarantees diversity, the peaceful transfer of powers, a well-defined exercise of authority ..."**

To all these principles, a vote of **"yes"** was uttered by all aspirants to the presidency of Egypt. These were leaders of all parties and various fields of

---

[78] Gamal El-Banna, <u>Diversity in Muslim Society</u> (Cairo, Dar Al-Fikr Al-Islami, 2001), p.3.

[79] Al-Azhar Declaration of August 17, 2011, as translated by this author.

thought, all opinion-makers of various stripes, including the Coptic leadership. It was an open conclave which was seated at the rectangular table of Dr. El-Taiyeb, the Grand Imam of Al-Azhar. Diversity was the winner.

The solidity of diversity in Islamic law is anchored in the Quran itself. It also manifests itself in Islam's advocacy of freedom of thought and expression, unfortunately contradicted by both jihadism and Wahhabism. The Quran states: **"There is no compulsion in Religion;"**[80] and addressing Muhammad, it goes on saying: **"You are not responsible for guiding them, but God guides whoever He pleases."**[81]

And in an emphasis on the direct relationship between the Creator and his creation, the Quran, again addresses the Messenger by saying: **"And say: 'The Truth is from your Lord, let him who will believe, and let him who will reject it.'"**[82]

So from where do jihadists get their lunatic ideology of dividing humanity into believers and non-believers? The only plausible answer is that their reality contorts itself into a sick imagination. This in turn is one of the strongest reasons for legitimating the new Islamic religious revolution. Its forefront leadership is at Al-Azhar of today. Its Grand Imam has often raised the importance of diversity in his several speeches in Europe, west and east, as well as in Africa. The following are brief samples.

Before the German Bundestag, Dr. El-Taiyeb declared Islam's commitment to diversity. Casting himself as a neutral explainer of Islam, he said: **"I am only a Muslim who loves all humanity , concerned with the issues of peace in all its religious, social and universalistic angles. I seek that peace and wish it for people, all people, regardless of the differences between their homelands, their races, their national identities, their religions, their systems of belief, and their schools of thought."**[83]

The same emphasis on diversity could be found in the statement by Sheikh

---

[80] <u>The Quran</u>, Chapter 2, Verse 256.

[81] <u>Ibid</u>, Verse 272.

[82] <u>The Quran</u>, Chapter 18, Verse 29.

[83] El-Taiyeb, Speech before the Bundestag, Berlin, March 15, 2016.

Al-Azhar at the East-West Dialogue of Scholars, made in June 2016. On that occasion, Dr. El-Taiyeb said: **"God's universal laws put justice and equality amongst all human beings at the forefront. These laws set forth their brotherhood, because they all have one father and one mother. Whatever divisions and differences between them through a heavenly will are differences of diversity, of getting to know one another, and of brotherhood."**[84]

How far removed are these lofty principles of the new Islamic religious revolution from the ethos of the Trumpist regressive revolt!! A revolt which rears its racist head through bigoted immigration policies. Such ethnic nationalism cannot possibly make America safe. It plays directly into the jihadist propaganda machine. The elements of this anti-humanitarian return to the dark ages could be encapsulated in the following policy elements.

Racism ascendant. Its manifestation is the mantra of **"America First."** Translation, at least in perceptual terms: **"America is for the whites only."**

Fusion, is a national necessity. What does **"fusion"** mean? To the new arrivals, forget the culture from which you came. Be **"an American"** by being comprehensively acculturated by and to American ways. Integration, a la Canadian way, is erroneously considered repugnant. That is because it safeguards **"the old ways."** There is nothing, so conveys Trumpism, that America can learn from **"the old world."**

Regional organizations, such as the European Union, and other international partnerships, such as the Trans-Pacific Partnership, and the North American Free Trade Agreement, are anathema to the national order. They uphold open borders, free trade, freedom of movements of people, goods and services. All, so claims anti-diversity advocates, are retardants of job growth and sovereign action.

Such retrograde policies have been expressed through what Charles M Blow, of the New York Times characterizes as **"degradation of the language."**[85]

---

[84] ______, Speech in Paris, at the East-West Dialogue of Scholars, June, 2016.

[85] Charles M. Blow, "Degradation of the Language," op. ed., The New York Times, May 1, 2017, p.A23.

Against such threatening background, the new Islamic religious revolution rises on the platform of diversity, with its companion platform of freedom of belief. The two platforms are mutually reinforcing. Both the jihadists and Trumpists deny the value of diversity, although the jihadists are more vocal than their ideological allies in their opposition to **"the freedom of belief."**

The most important quality of **"belief"** is that it resides in the heart. Non-negotiable. The Quran exhorts as follows: **"Whoever is guided, is guided only for his own soul, and whoever goes astray, he is astray only for his own soul, and I am not a trustee over you."**[86] Thus even Muhammad is not regarded as a belief-controller. In the same vein, the Quran stresses over and over again that right to freedom of belief. It states: **"Whoever takes the righteous way, his righteousness is for his own good; and whoever goes astray, it is for his own loss alone. No soul bears the burden of another."** [87] No collective guilt.

In these Quranic assertions, one would have to logically extrapolate the following standards which now permeate the new Islamic revolution. First: freedom of belief, as stated above. Second: The right to that freedom is personal. Third: Even the Prophet Muhammad has neither the role nor the authority, to be the decider of such issues of the heart. Fourth: Conduct, acts or action, by one individual is incapable of establishing collective responsibility. Fifth: The direct relationship between every human and their Creator.

This is the kind of freedom which underpins diversity -the variables which are the total make-up of a humanity on the move. The propellor of that move is divergences which enlighten one another in a texture of various colors and strands. Thus there exists a ravine between these Islamic law concepts and the fascist ideology of terror organizations which call for uniformity along murderous lines of their fabricated **"Islam."**

The direct result of that kind of fascism has been the depiction, especially in the West, of Islam as a cult. The vicious circle of an ISIS ideology, becomes fodder for the grist of the media mill. Then it returns back to those terror organizations, recycled in the form of **"Islam-haters."**

Breaking that cycle is now one of the central objectives of Al-Azhar as it

---

[86] <u>The Quran</u>, Chapter 10, Verse 108.

[87] __________, Chapter 15, Verse 15.

goes forward with the unfurled banner of the new Islamic religious revolution. Dr. Ahmed El-Taiyeb speaks out addressing this issue at the opening session for the convention of Islamic scholars, held in Cairo in 2017.

On that occasion, the Grand Imam of Al-Azhar said: **"It is enough for one to discern this rag-tag group as it raises one flag, the flag of Islam. Only to turn against one another with charges of treason and apostasy. You shall then certainly realize that there is nothing in their entire case which has anything to do with faith. The conclusion is that they employ Islam as an instrument of blood in several ways which oscillate from one contradiction to another."**[88]

That oscillation and these contradictions within the jihadi sphere are the very targets of the new Islamic revolution in its attempt to weaken, then end this charade. The global reflection of this tug of war has been made abundantly clear from the impact of the flood of Muslim refugees on the shores of Europe and America. The rise of **"no Islamization of Europe"** as a movement owes its success largely to the confrontation between Islam versus jihadism.

In this regard, the examples of Great Britain and France are instructive. In the UK we have Brexit, and in the French elections of May 7, 2017 we have Marie Le Pen. 36% for Le Pen; nearly double that for Emmanuel Macron. The Macron victory seems to arrest the European race to the bottom.

Macron, at the age of 39, has been a **"strong advocate of a free market: has called for France to be more innovative and focus on getting benefits from globalization."**[89] In his victory speech, Macron vowed to **"rebuild the relationship between Europe and the peoples that make it."**[90] It is diversity which makes the people of Europe.

Diversity being central to universality has twin roots in Islam. One geographic: Judaism, Christianity, and Islam were born contiguously in the

---

[88] El-Taiyeb, Speech before the convention of Islamic scholars held in Cairo in 2017.

[89] "Macron prepares to shake up France," <u>Toronto Star</u>, Toronto, Canada, March 9, 2017, p. A2.

[90] Id.

MIddle East.

The other spiritual. The logic of right and wrong cannot apply to faith evaluation. Every faith represents particular human needs for knowing the raison d'etre of its existence. **"Why am I on earth?"** has been the primordial question lurking in the back of the human mind. The search for a purpose. Hence the differentiation between religions whose adherents may be different, but their spiritual needs are anchored to a higher purpose -one and common at the same time.

That diversity in the context of universality has always been an Islamic ideological pillar. It allocated religious differences to the environments in which they existed. But kept the judgment to be issued on them firmly in the hands of God. For **"God has kept in his hands the resolution of those differences on judgement day."**[91] Thus the Quran settled the issue of disagreement as it denied to every protagonist any claim to superiority… That is not for resolution by individuals."[92]

A former Grand Imam of Al-Azhar, Sheikh Mahmoud Shaltout had authored a book titled **"Islam: Faith and Law."** In that seminal work, Imam Shaltout said: **"Those who do not believe in God (in Arabic - Allah) and in his messengers cannot be subjected to the laws governing Muslims in their relationships to God or amongst themselves. This exemption does not connote that they are infidels destined to an eternal banishment in hell."**[93]

Imam Shaltout then goes on to nail down the import of that exemption for non-Muslims in these words: **"Since they are not subjected in this life to Islamic law and rules (in Arabic, Ahkam), they are not called upon to follow Muslim religious practices; they are free from the Islamic injunction against drinking alcohol, eating pork, or trading in such products."**[94]

---

[91] Gamal El-Banna, <u>Diversity In an Islamic Society</u> (Cairo: Dar Al-Fikr Al-Arabi, 2001).

[92] Id.

[93] Quoted in Ib<u>id</u>, p.32.

[94] Id.

These principles are lucidly enunciated in Al-Azhar's attacks against the destructive calls by jihadis for total conformity. This is a retrograde interpretation of an Islam of the sword, by the sword, and for the sword. The sword is their revered tool which emblazons the emblem of the Muslim Brotherhood, and the flag of Saudi Arabia, not as a kingdom but as a Wahhabi citadel. A citadel into which no bibles can be imported, no churches or synagogues can be built. This is while they generously fund the building of mosques and the delivering of tons of shipments of the Quran all over the word. A very uneven relationship.

There is another angle of diversity as a central tenet of the new Islamic religious revolution. Oneness, being the opposite of diversity, has been reserved only to God. Tawheed, in Arabic, is a hallowed term as it stands for that oneness. In the Quran, there are 99 names which refer to God. Among them are these two names: **"The One"** (Al-Wahid), and **"the unique One"** (Al-Ahad).

Such references in the Quran to God have, by that revered and inspired text, preempted the field of uniqueness. That preemption leaves to all of humanity only **"diversity"** as a **modus operandi.** A diversity which may be reflected in all religious symbols, statues, icons, practices, church bells, vestments as the IDs of all other faiths.

Thus when Islamic scholars and others say that **"Sharia (Islamic law) is fit for all times and places,"** it does not mean Islamization of the world. Adopting this **"world Islamization"** as a battle cry against 1.7 billion Muslims is not only a disservice to the proper knowledge of Islam. It is an ideological spur for jihadis to pursue their ungodly rampage using **"the war on Islam"** as their mantra.

The riposte against this jihadi lunacy was articulated by Dr. El-Taiyeb in his speech at Abuja, Nigeria, in May 2016. In the presence of Nigeria's President Bouhrai, the Grand Imam of Al-Azhar said: **"We preserve in our hearts the famous Islamic rule: 'What was legislated for those who preceded the age of Islam is also applicable to us Muslims, unless textually abrogated."**

The appearance of Dr. El-Taiyeb in Nigeria was significant. For many years, Nigeria has been the land of the rampage by Boko Haram. The largest African country, demographically, it's great Muslim North is inhabited by 60% of the Nigerian population of more than 200 million. Boko Haram, a jihadi affiliate of ISIS, stands as a name for **"Western learning is sinful."** And as a movement, its repeated attacks on Maindaugry in the north-east has spread fear and displacement.

Boko Haram, which is in the cross-hairs of the new Islamic revolution has been targeting the most vulnerable of the Muslim population -women. The tragedy of Chibok, Nigeria, where 300 schoolgirls were kidnapped in 2014 has caused world-wide revulsion. Jihadis regard females as unequal to males. Rape is a jihadi weapon of societal destruction. At 9 years of age, these young Nigerian women are brutalized as **"jihadi slave wives,"** as combatants, and as **"suicide bombers."** On May 6, 2017, 80 of those victims were released. A hundred of them remain in jihadi bondage.[95]

The question then arises: Can't governments unite their efforts to end, through arms and ideology, the present dark age of Boko Haram, ISIS, the Friends of Jerusalem, and the lunatic core of the Muslim Brotherhood? In theory, yes. But in effect, in today's age of the individual, governments as well as international and regional organizations, need community involvement.

Communal involvement, across the spectrum of diversity, has become an indispensable ingredient in pushing back against those murderous ideologies, now raging under the cover of a misunderstood Islam. In turn, that communal involvement needs to be brought on board through learning about religious verities and falsehoods, training in how to detect early ominous signs of radicalization. There is a need to know how to cooperate with the police and other security forces, without breaking the bonds between neighborhoods. In essence, it is the operationalization of **"If you see something, say something."**

Herein lies the dangers of **"Muslim bans."** Those are uninformed Trumpist tools of walling the danger of terrorism out, while, as has been revealed in numerous instances, the danger also lurks from within. One can never pretend that the anti-jihadi fight is winnable in the short term. It promises to be a long struggle, but the effort cannot be given up. Resilience, in the face of evil, is a strategic necessity.

Diversity being central to universality, is an effective weapon in this world-wide combat. Patience is its weaponized endurance. In World War II no less than 40 millions perished including on the battlefield, in Nazi concentration camps, or as hapless civilians in Dresden (Germany), Hiroshima and Nagasaki (Japan).

---

[95] <u>Toronto Star</u>, Toronto, Canada, May 6, 2017.

The Quran urges patience in the fight against the enemies of the freedom of belief. It says: **"And many Messengers before you (Muhammad) were disbelieved, but they were patient and constant when so disbelieved and harmed, until our help came to them."**[96] **This is the basic mission of the new Islamic religious revolution.**

---

[96] The Quran, Chapter 6, Verse 34.

CHAPTER 9

Popular Consultation (SHURA) As A Democratic Mechanism

The Quran names an entire chapter of its 114 chapters **"Shura-Consultation."** It says: **"And those who respond to their Lord and establish prayer, and who on matters other than those God has decreed, conduct them by mutual consultation…"**[97]

As popular consultation, the Quran again stresses it as a popular means, in effect a democratic mechanism, for ascertaining public opinion. In Chapter 3, it advises Muhammad to conduct himself in his advocacy in a communicative manner. It says: **"It was by God's Mercy that you were kind to them; had you been harsh and hard of heart, they would have dispersed from around you. So pardon them, and pray for forgiveness for them. And consult them in the matter, and when you reach a decision, place your trust in God; surely God loves those who put their trust in Him."**[98]

The role of consultation in Islamic jurisprudence is historic in the sense of its being pre-Islamic. The reign of Islam began 1400 years ago in a highly tribalized society. Conflict was the norm; reconciliation through the intervention of a wise person was an acceptable mode. With Islam, the Quran, consisting of more than 6000 verses (ayas), was revealed in both Mecca and Medina.[99]

---

[97] The Quran, Chapter 42, Verse 38.

[98] Ibid., Chapter 3, Verse 159

[99] Ahmed Amin, The Dawn of Islam (Fajr Al-Islam) (Beirut, Dar Al-Kotob Al-

Two-thirds of those verses were Meccan, and largely dealt with faith; one third were Medinan, of which only 200 were of a legal nature. The State began in Medinah, the legal rules were new, the jockeying for power between the Meccans (generally called the immigrants -Al-Muhajeroon) and the Medinans (generally called the supporters -Al-Ansar) was forever present. WIthin the vortex of that mix, consultation (Shura) became ascendant.

A historic adage was uttered by Abu-Bakr, the first caliph (successor) after Muhammad. When elected to lead the new Islamic Ummah (community) he called on the Muslims: **"If I err, set me straight."**[100] The main purpose of consultation (shura) is to ascertain in a conciliar fashion where the public good lies as perceived by its beneficiaries.

From early Islamic history, the scope of shura was both comprehensive and principled. As a mechanism it involved the community which was made to understand the principles guiding their opinion-voicing. The new Islamic religious revolution, in highlighting a variety of paths towards democracy, does not miss the earliest of episodes which illustrate the cogency of Shura.

One such episode is that about Abu-Bakr attempting to cede land not fit for cultivation to two tribal bedouins. The land seekers had convinced the First Caliph that they would reclaim that land to productivity. Based on that reasoning, he gave them a deed but conditioned it on its being witnessed by Omar Ibn Al-Khattab who later succeeded him as the Second Caliph. But Omar tore up the deed and later explained to Abu-Bakr that **"The Prince of the Faithful"** had erred in not involving the entire community in ceding public land to only two members of that community."[101]

The conceptual link to this hallowed tradition is manifest in **"Al-Azhar Document on Egypt's Future."** Dated May 19, 2011, seven months following the Egyptian Revolution of January 25, 2011, its first principle read as follows: **"Egypt as a State is based upon a constitutional**

---

ilmiyah, 2009), pp. 220-221, 3rd edition.

[100] Dr. Isamail Al-Daftar, Imam of the Amre Ibn El-As Mosque, Cairo, Egypt. Transcript of Friday sermon, Dec. 16, 2005, p.1 (author's translation). (Hereinafter cited as: Al-Daftar's Sermons).

[101] Ibid., p.2.

democracy with separation of powers, of which the legislative power is to be exercised by the people's representatives."[102] This document was also endorsed by the Coptic Church.

Again the preamble of the secular Egyptian Constitution of 2014, which amended the Islamic Constitution of 2012, stated: **"We believe in democracy as a path, a future and a way of life, including political diversity, and the peaceful transfer of power. We also emphasize the people's right to fashion its future, as they alone are the source of all powers, because human freedom and dignity and social justice all constitute the right of each citizen and of future generations to sovereignty in a sovereign homeland."**[103]

That continuum of the shura principle was again, and repeatedly, expounded by the Grand Imam of Al-Azhar, Dr. El-Taiyeb, in his 2016 statements in Europe and Africa. At the Bundestag (Berlin), he addressed the European Parliament in March 2016 stating, among other principles, the following: **"Islamic Sharia"** (Law) is anchored in the principles of justice, equality, freedom, and human dignity. The Prophet of Islam has advocated the principle of equality amongst people at a time when the human thinking could neither digest, nor comprehend, nor visualize this principle… And when the Second Caliph, Omar Ibn Al-KHattab assumed the leadership, he screamed in the face of an Islamic ruler (of Egypt): **"When have you enslaved the people to whom their mothers have given birth as free people?"**[104]

In another Al-Azhar document entitled, **"In Support of The Arab People's Will,"** issued on October 30, 2011, Al-Azhar, with the full endorsement of a galaxy of intellectuals, made an important clarification. It was in response to the abuse of understanding of a Quranic verse. That verse said: **"O you who believe! Obey God and obey the Messenger (Muhammad), and those entrusted with authority over you."**[105]

---

[102] "Al-Azhar Document on Egypt's Future," May 19, 2011. (Author's translation from the original Arabic.)

[103] The Egyptian Constitution of 2014, As promulgated by Interim President Judge Adly Mansour, on January 2014. Preamble. (Author's translation from the original Arabic.)

[104] El-Taiyeb's speech at the Bundestag, March 2016. (Author's translation).

[105] The Quran, Chapter 4, Verse 59.

Arab and Muslim rulers who governed dictatorially outside of the shura framework anchored their authority in that misunderstood verse. The history of abuse of this verse stretched from the Umayyad dynasty (7th century AD), to Saddam Hussein, to the Islamic reign of the Muslim Brotherhood in Egypt (2012-2013). More ominously, it inspired the jihadi narrative of brutal exclusivity of a retrograde type of Sunni rule.

The corrective narrative, advocated in the above-referenced Al-Azhar document, pointed to the verse immediately preceding the abused verse in the same Chapter. It reads: **"Indeed! God commands you to render back trusts to whom they belong. And when you judge between people, that you judge with justice."**[106] Taking this into account, the Al-Azhar document puts the entire argument in the context of the new Islamic revolutionary movement.

Such assertions denote rulership as a trust in the very way of Montesquieu's thesis in his book **The Spirit of the Laws (1748),** and Voltaire's **The Philosophical Dictionary (1764).** It is so with shura in Islamic practice as a reflection of the social contract -an agreement between the governed and the government defining the rights and duties of each. Akin to the thesis of Jean Jacque Rousseau in his historic book, **The Social Contract.**

The shura's importance is also cast by the Prophet Muhammad as a religious duty. Muhammad defined religion in simple terms. **"Religion is a counsel rendered."** In another Hadith, he said: **"it is the duty of a Muslim toward another Muslim to offer advice when asked for it."** In this connection, counsel is an advice given especially as a result of consultation.

In Islamic Law, no ruler is infallible. An erring ruler has to be called on his error. The Second Caliph, Omar Ibn Al-Khattab whose statement on the judiciary appears at nearly every Egyptian Court has encouraged shura as a corrective mechanism. He is reputed to have said: **"If you don't render it, you shall garner no good. And if we don't abide by it, we (as rulers) garner no good either."**[107]

Furthermore, there is a nexus between shura and an oath of allegiance

---

[106] Ibid, Chapter 4, Verse 58.

[107] As quoted in Al-Daftar's Sermons, December 9, 2005, p.9.

(bayaa). The former leads to the latter as it provides for an informed public opinion. **"The traditional oath of allegiance (bayaa) should now be seen as an authoritative basis for mutual contract between the government and the population at large."**[108]

We also see in the Shura a dividing line between Salafi-Jihadism and the new Islamic religious revolution. Whereas the latter sees in shura a democratic mechanism, the former proposes diminishing the role of consultative bodies. Jihadism leaves **"the head of State free to dismiss mainstream opinions on issues where they have adopted an alternative view."**[109]

This advocacy of **"an alternative view"** of governances as centered into the hands of one strong executive is made concrete by ISIS in Syria and Iraq. **"The alleged Caliphate currently operating in parts of Syria and Iraq is run in this way with its leader, Abu Bakr al-Baghdadi, adopting unilateral opinions which then bind his citizens."**[110] This should be contrasted to the freedom of voicing a contrary opinion, even in councils held by the Prophet Muhammad.

The jihadi/Salafi rational collapses the entire Shura concept and practice. This is because they believe that **"canonical authority resides not in individuals but in scriptures, the Quran and the sunna."** As to how these sources of scripture are best interpreted at the political level, the jihadis oppose the mainstream islamists who call for a robust role for consultation (Shura). In their opposition to the advocacy on this point by the new Islamic revolution, the Salafi-jihadis insist on a monopolistic role for the Caliph. The jihadi argument stands in full opposition to the very words of the Quran.

In this connection, the Quran devotes a full Chapter (#58) to a pleading, an argument, voiced by a woman disputing the legality of her divorce to the Prophet himself. **"Allah has indeed heard and accepted the statement of the woman who pleads with you concerning her husband, and**

---

[108] Abdullahi Ahmed An-Na'im, <u>Islam and the Secular State: Negotiating The Future of Sharia </u>(Cambridge: Harvard University Press, 2008), p.110.

[109] Shiraz Maher, <u>Salafi-Jihadism: The History of an Idea</u> (New York: Oxford University Press, 2016), p. 193.

[110] <u>Id</u>.

carries her complaint (in prayer) to Allah. And Allah always hears the arguments between both sides among you. For Allah hears and sees all things."[111]

As has been noted above, there is nothing in Islamic jurisprudence which accepts the legality of a dictatorial governance. There is no religious or legal basis for the jihadi belief that **Allah's sovereignty can only be realized through absolute obedience to the ruler.** The unislamic jihadi belief in that blind dictatorship, devoid of any form of consultation for the ascertainment of the popular will, has been at the root of the havoc caused by ISIS, Al-Qaeda, and their affiliates, throughout the entire world.

The fallacy of that belief, called discipline, becomes apparent in the denial of the freedom of expression and of belief which is symptomatic of Islamic law. The jihadi thesis is that **"Allah has entrusted them with power; (thus) they are the rulers chosen by God, and it is therefore incumbent upon people to obey them even if they are oppressive."**[112]

In this regard, jihadism parallels the thesis of the Muslim Brotherhood as it contests the legitimacy of the ouster of former Egyptian President Mohamed Morsi. My blog posting of May 29, 2017 dealt with that issue under the title of **"Series of Failed Mischief By the Muslim Brotherhood In Egypt and Abroad."**[113] Collapsing the regime of the Brotherhood in Egypt (2012-2013) had widening ripple effects throughout the Middle East. Reference is made here to the blog posting of May 29, 2017 where it stated:
"With the Egyptian arena preempted by secularism, the Muslim Brotherhood is in **hot pursuit for life support overseas.** *Their megaphones, whether in Qatar, Turkey, or America, produce echo chambers. Collapsing the New Egypt is nothing but a pipe dream."*

The case against dictatorship being acceptable to Islamic law has been dismissed since the time of the Prophet Muhammad. Aside from the Quranic references listed above, here is an authenticated saying (hadith) by Muhammad. **"Amongst people, the most beloved to God is a just ruler,**

---

[111] The Quran, Chapter 58, Verse 1

[112] Maher, op. Cit., p.193.

[113] http://tahrirforever.blogspot.com

and the most rejected is an unjust ruler."[114]

Although shura is not the equivalent of elections, yet as an early form in Islamic society of a path to democracy cannot be underestimated. WIth the great diversity of Muslim lands, cultures and practices, this recognition of shura as a facet of introducing the new Islamic religious revolution has its merited place.

---

[114] As quoted by this author in a lecture delivered before the Egyptian Council For Foreign Affairs (ECFA), Cairo, Egypt on May 17, 2006. In Arabic.

CHAPTER 10

The Caliphate: Non-Authentic After Imam Ali (661 AD)

Evidence is non-existing regarding the legitimacy of Caliphas since the assassination of Imam Ali Ibn Abi-Taleb in 661 AD. The only legitimate Caliphas are the first four who succeeded the Prophet Muhammad. These are Abu Bakr, Omar, Othman and Ali. On that basis, the period of usurpation of that title has stretched from the Ummayad dynasty (661-750 AD) in Damascus, through the Abbasids in Baghdad (750-1258 AD), overlapping the Fatimids and Saladin (the Ayoubis) (1169-1250 AD).

From then on, from Arab-Persian based caliphates to the brutal assumption of that religious-secular title by the Turkic successors, including the Ottoman Caliphate, we find no authentication. Neither through Islamic Law, nor a secularly-sanctioned popular will. The elimination of the Ottoman (Turkish) Caliphate by Ata Turk in 1923 has put a final end to this charade in Muslim governance.

Thus when a thug from Anbar, Iraq, Abu-Bakr Al-Baghdadi declared himself, upon splitting from Al-Qaeda in 2014, as Calipha of all Muslims, with Raqqa, Syria, being the capital, one reaches the bottom of the barrel of heinous fabrication. The end of that terrible joke came through the force of arms in the summer of 2017 in both Mosul (Iraq) and Raqqa, (Syria). A most welcome riddance.

In the Quran, there are evidences, though indirect, on what is Islamically permissible as a title for Calipha (successor). The Quran says: **"O David, We have appointed you Khalifa on the earth, so judge between the people with justice, and do not follow vain desires, lest it leads you**

astray from the Way of God."[115] In other translations of the Quran, **"Khalifa"** or **"Calipha"** is translated **"vicegerent"** (one who rules or manages).[116]

The legitimation of the first four Caliphas succeeding the Prophet Muhammad is based on their direct linkage to the Prophet. Such linkage was enhanced by the process of recommendation from one to another from Muhammad to Othman. As to Ali, it was by a popular draft (Bayaa)(656-661 AD). This chain of linkages came to an end in 661 AD, when Imam Ali was assassinated in Kufa (Iraq). From the Ummayads (usurping the Caliphate in 661 AD, down to Ataturk in Constantinople, ending the Ottoman Caliphate (1299-1923), those were regimes calling themselves successors of the Prophet. No authentication, as the chain was broken as of 661 AD. Auto-naming themselves as Caliphates was intended only to bestow outward legitimacy.

Ali's reign, as the last **"enlightened"** of the four Caliphates began in a few days from the assassination of his predecessor Othman in 656 AD. The shedding of Othman's blood, sparked the first inter-Islamic civil war. The Ummayads, whose tribe Bani Ummyah came to Islam late, having been defeated combattants at the hands of the adherents of Islam, were sheer usurpers. Theirs was a monarchical regime. So were the Abbasids (750-1258) who moved the capital from Damascus to Baghdad. In a matter of 200 years following the destruction of the Abbasid Caliphate, the pretended Caliphs were non-Arabs (Turkic races) who used the sword as a weapon of suppression until the end of their least-enlightened empire. Calling themselves **"Ottomans"** have nothing to do with Othman, the third Enlightened Caliph. That name, Othman, referred to their Turkish founder (Othman Artaghral).

Even the intervening Caliphate of the Fatimids (the name links them to Ali's spouse, Fatima Al-Zahra, Muhammad's daughter) had no ascertainable link to the Prophet Muhammad and the first Four succeeding him. A Shii dynasty born in North Africa (909 to 1171 AD), and sweeping eastward to Egypt, Palestine and Syria, their cultural contribution (e.g. the establishment of Cairo and of Al-Azhar mosque in the late 970s) creates no pretence to Caliphate legitimacy. No linkage to the enlightened caliphates residing in

---

[115] The Quran, Chapter 38, Verse 26.

[116] Abdullah Yusuf Ali, The Glorious Quran Translation (Delhi: Amir Printing Press, 2006).

Medina and Kofa, from the passing of Muhammad till the assassination of Ali.

The Fatimids reign was ended by Salah El-Din (Saladin), a Kurd who established the Ayyubid dynasty (1169-1250 AD), thus began Sunnism in Egypt. From the Ayyubids, who vanquished the Crusaders, the procession of false caliphates was then led by the Mamelukes (white slaves and soldiers) from 1250 AD until the Ottoman reign in the 16th century.

So when ISIS, a terrorist organization, calls itself a Caliphate, that sheer hoax is intended to seek undeserved legitimation. That is regardless of its leader Abu-Bakr Al-Baghdadi, setting on a journey of global criminality in the name of an Islamic Caliphate. Neither he, nor Al-Qaeda of Bin Laden, from which he split for power purposes, have any standing. Neither in the history of the true Caliphates, nor in the ideological content of Al-Azhar, the main citadel of Islamic learning, which is forging ahead with its New Islamic Religious Revolution.

Dr. El-Taiyeb, the Rector of Al-Azhar, does not mince his words as he delegitimizes those marauding maniacs. In Abuja, Nigeria, he declared in May 2016: **"It would not have occurred to Muslims, scholars or non-scholars, that the day would come when they would be obliged to tour the world to defend their faith or to clarify its substance and reality."**

Then he went on to say: **"A band of those claiming to adhere to Islam have unjustly and fraudulently put that faith in the dark. They have besmirched its beautiful face, and sullied its clear and lofty image by blood and human flesh. They have made sure to broadcast and telecast scenes of head-cutting with noted insistence on savagery the likes of which has not been seen throughout human history... They had but only one objective: Global defamation of Islam."**[117]

Against the background of such authoritative delegitimation, what is left for us to be called a Caliphate? Nothing!! The essence of authentication of the Four Enlightened Caliphs was **"justice"** and law observance. Without such qualification, there is no Caliphate. Islam created, not a State, but a community (Ummah) in the context of popular acceptance and trust. This was one of the central reasons for Egypt throwing the Muslim Brotherhood

---

[117] El-Taiyeb speech in Abuja, Nigeria (May 2016). My translation from the original Arabic.

out of power (2012-2013). Without an observed **"social contract"** (a la Jean Jacque Rousseau) between the ruler and the ruled, there is no governance legitimacy.

The central theme of Muhammad's message is reform. It is the betterment of society. Any governance mode which ignores that message goes against the grain of Islam as essentially a system of justifiable transactions. The Quran points this out, as it speaks on behalf of the Prophet Muhammad. It declares: **"I do not wish, in opposition to you, to do that which I forbid you to do. I only desire your betterment to the best of my power. And my success in my task can only come from Allah. To Him I trust and to Him I look."**[118]

Those twin pillars of Islam as derived from the Quran and the Sunna, namely, faith and Sharia (Islamic law), were never fully functioning since the assassination of Imam Ali Ibn Abi-Taleb in 661 AD. Calling the Islamic regimes which came thereafter **"Caliphates,"** is intrinsically misleading. Whether these were the Ummayads or the Abhasids or the Fatimides or the Ottomans. None of these Caliphates deserves that name. Least of all, the ISIS so-called caliphate, under the phony leadership of Abu-Bakr Al-Baghdadi.

As a human liberation movement, with links to all faiths, Islam has placed **"justice"** on top of the list of governing pre-requisites. No justice, no Islam. Reinforcing the primacy of justice in Islamic jurisprudence, Chapter 12 in the Quran cites 99 names for God. One such name is Al-Aadel (The Just).

To the above, we should add that Islamic practices do not require unnecessary structures. And because a caliphate is a superstructure of a hierarchical nature, it is an abysmal development for two reasons: It is an authority which defines the nature of both faith and State; and it is an impediment to one of the basic tenets of Islam -**"freedom of thought."**

In as much as any Caliphate established after 661 AD is a central mechanism whose aim is its own legitimation through a link to the Four Enlightened Caliphs (Abu-Bakr, Omar, Othman, and Ali), it chokes off that unique and direct relationships between the human and God. On that point, the Quran says: **"Say, 'O people, surely there has come to you the Truth from your Lord: whoever is guided, is guided only for his**

---

[118] The Quran, Chapter 11, Verse 88.

own soul. And whoever goes astray, he is astray only for his own soul, and I am not a trustee over you."[119]

The Quran therefore is repeatedly emphatic on the direct relationship in matters of faith between man and God. No intermediary. In another Chapter, it declares: **"And every Messenger We have sent, We made him convey the Message in the language of his people; that he might make all matters clear to them. Then God leaves astray whoever He pleases, and guides whoever He pleases. And He is the Almighty, the All-wise."**[120]

Such Quranic clarifications have been encapsulated in the general Islamic adage that **"Deliverance comes from within."** It does not come from a caliphate. Thus Islamic law, while stressing law and order through governance emerging from the will of the people (e.g. Shura), it leaves no room for a hierarchy like a Caliphate that looks upon itself as the monopolistic interpreter of faith.

The Ottoman Empire has proven the inimical nature of a caliphate to the law and spirit of Islam. Its claim to religious sanctity is wholly deceptive. Its reliance on the sword, its resort to paramountcy through limited suzerainty over the holy places of Mecca and Medina, and its oppression in the Balkans and the Arab vast area, are all testimony to the acuity of a Caliphate substance. In Islamic jurisprudence, this was a kingdom without a throne.

In the post real and only recognizable caliphates (the first Four Enlightened Caliphs), the use of fear of social strife as a weapon, resulting from disobedience of the presumptive caliphates, proves the point. Oppression produces strife which cannot be contained by the enhancement of that oppression. The new Islamic revolution denies the authenticity of the argument that **"Allah's sovereignty can only be realized through absolute obedience to the ruler."**[121]

Obedience, jihad and reform (islah) are a toxic mix. That mix being a jihadi hoax is now being exploded by Al-Azhar's attack on its validity. In its document of October 30, 2011, issued in the aftermath of the Egyptian

---

[119] Ibid, Chapter 10, Verse 108.

[120] Ibid, Chapter 14, Verse 4.

[121] Maher, op. Cit., p. 193. See also Chapter 12 of this volume below.

Revolution of January 2011, Al-Azhar strikes back. With no reference whatsoever to a caliphate, that document, issued jointly by Al-Azhar with the consensus of liberal scholars and the Coptic Church, it makes a central argument.

Section II of that document reflects the heart of the thesis contained in its title **"In support of the popular will of the Arab people."** It states, **inter alia,** that **"Whenever the rulers remain unresponsive to the call of their people… for liberty, justice and equity, the patriotic opposition to those rulers cannot be described as "the oppressors." From the perspective of Islamic jurisprudence (fiqh), the oppressors are those who wield power over their people from whom they are totally isolated."**[122]

Such arguments, emerging from Al-Azhar in the wake of the Egyptian twin revolutions (2011 and 2013) lead us to additional conclusions. None of these conclusions support the concept of a caliphate. The right to self-determination of every country and every **"people,"** as affirmed, among others, by the American President Woodrow Wilson at the Paris Peace Conference of 1919, argues against a transnational caliphate. The simple definition of an empire is a transnational state.

Such a historic affirmation, a part of Wilson's **"Fourteen Points,"** was at the time pronounced when the Ottoman Empire was breathing its last. Its formal end came in 1923 with Ata Turk unilaterally declaring the end of the Caliphate. He rightly regarded it as a retardant to the modernization of Turkey. At present, Turkey, under President Ordogan, seems to be moving backward, from a secular State to an Islamist State, in search of the rainbow, in fact, the falacy of national glory through a mythical Caliphate.

It is therefore axiomatic to discern the collision, ideologically and practically, between the new Islamic religious revolution and the latter-day emergence of brutal terrorism. A terrorism wearing the garb of the ISIS caliphate in Raqqa, Syria (2014-2017). It is also graphically symbolic that the short-lived inclusion of Mosul, Iraq, in that so-called Caliphate came to an end in June 2017 with the destruction of a Mosul mosque of 800-year old. From that pulpit, Al-Baghdadi has announced the illegitimate birth of his short-lived caliphate. That act of destruction was done by ISIS itself as the Iraqi forces closed on in for the final kill.

---

[122] Documents issued by Al-Azhar Al-Shareef, Document #2, p.32 (2012). In Arabic. Author's translation.

The rise and fall of ISIS as a transnational structure, demonstrates the uses of a caliphate as a vehicle of oppression in the name of Islam. Addressing Nigeria, where Boko Horam has been entrenched, Dr. El-Taiyeb of Al-Azhar went through a detailed analysis of how Islam and terrorism can never mix.

In his advocacy in Abuja, Nigeria, Sheikh Ahmed El-Taiyeb, declared that true Islam was humane, a faith of peace and security, both regionally and universally. The culmination of that advocacy was: **"The glorious Quran affirms the commonality between the Islamic message and pre-Islamic messages in substance, fact, and context. Allah did not inspire the Muslims with a new faith. He inspired them with what He had inspired prior prophets, messengers and nations."**[123]

On this continuum of faith, the Grand Imam of Al-Azhar quoted from the Quran as saying: **"He has ordained for you the Religion which He Commanded to Noah, and that We have revealed to you, and that which We Commanded to Abraham, and Moses, and Jesus: 'Establish the Religion, and be not divided therein.'"**[124]

In the context of that continuity of faith, stands Tawheed (the Oneness of God) as the common denominator. That oneness is also a guarantee for the individual's freedom of thought, of expression, and of faith. All of these are attributes which cannot be safeguarded within a caliphate coming after the end of the Ali caliphate in 661.

One of the recognized Islamic scholars, the late Gamal Al-Banna, stated **"Naturally, within the freedom of thought and of belief, there is also the freedom of changing of faith including religion. Some Muslim scholars call for the freedom of thought, but reject the freedom to change faith."**[125] Then he cites the Quran as stating: **"(Addressing Muhammad) And if your Lord had pleased, whoever is on the earth would have believed, all of them together. Would you then compel**

---

[123] El-Taiyeb speech in Abuja, Nigeria, May 2016. Author's translation from the original Arabic.

[124] The Quran, Chapter 42, Verse 13.

[125] Gamal Al-Banna, Our First Quest Is For Freedom, (Cairo, Dar Al-Fikr Al-Islami, 2000), p.6. In Arabic. Author's translation.

the people to become believers?"[126]

Supporting my thesis regarding the illegitimacy of the Caliphate after the reign of Imam Ali (661 AD) is a grand pioneer in the history of early Islam. Dr. Ahmed Amin, in his book entitled **"The Mid-Morning of Islam"** (Dhoda Al-Islam) says: **"In reality, the Ummayyad rule was not Islamic. This is because it did not treat its subjects as equal… The rulers were not at the service of the citizens. It was a governance in which the Arabs were loyal to their tribal heritage, not to Islam's directions."**[127]

Since 661 AD, the totalitarianism represented by the institution of the caliphate has suppressed all of these freedoms. It even made such suppression a religious calling whose refutation amounted to apostasy and insurrection. It is truly amazing that a humanly-created institution like the caliphate succeeded over the centuries to call for veneration. Over the years, that false call degenerated into ISIS and similar terror organizations.

---

[126] The Quran, Chapter 10, Verse 99.

[127] Ahmed Amin, The Mid-Morning of Islam (Dhoha Al-Islam) (Cairo: Maktabet Al-Nahdah Al-Misriyah, 1961), Vol. 1, 6th edition, p.27. In Arabic.

CHAPTER 11

The Myth of a Sunni Islam and a Shii Islam

Taha Hussein, one of the great thinkers in modern Arab history, wrote a book on Imam Ali Ibn Abi-Taleb. Imam Ali, cousin of the Prophet Muhammad and Muhammad's son-in-law, was the Fourth Enlightened Caliph, after the passing of the Prophet. His assassination in 661 AD ended the reign of Al-Cilapha as was discussed in Chapter 10 of this book. Only Abu-Bakr, the first of these four successors of Muhammad, died a natural death. The three who followed him, Omar, Othman, and Ali were assassinated.

The book referred to above by Taha Hussein, was appropriately titled **"The Greatest Insurrection."** That was in reference to the total chaos which afflicted the Muslim Ummah (community) as of the assassination of Othman. The book's sub-title is **"Ali and His Sons,"**[128] in reference to Ali's two sons, Al-Hassan and Al-Hussein. The two sons were also murdered by the Ummayads who illegally claimed the title of the Caliphate.

The thesis of this chapter is that the rise of Ali's partisans (Ali's Shiia) did not create a new type of Islam. There is no Sunni Islam or Shii Islam, but one Islam. That myth of religious differentiation between Sunnis (the followers of Muhammad's tradition) and Shiias (Ali's partisans) is a hoax. It has neither doctrinal nor theological basis. Its perpetuation, especially through the inimical relationship between the so-called Sunni States of the Gulf, and Shii Iran, on the eastern shores of the Gulf, has destabilized the

---

[128] Taha Hussein, <u>The Greatest Insurrection: Ali and His Sons</u> (Cairo: Dar Al-Maarif, 2006). Vol. 2.

region. The blame for that distancing between those Arab States and Iran is to be shared by the two sides.

That historic schism between Sunnis and Shia is now being targeted by the new Islamic religious revolution with the aim of ending it. Al-Azhar, established in Cairo by the Fatimids (shiis) in the latter part of the 10th century AD, is trying to remedy that rupture. It has included the School of the Twelvers (Shii) in its curriculum. That curriculum was previously limited to teaching the four Sunni Schools of Islam (Mazhabs). Such a start should be broadened in order to seep into the public culture and consciousness of the Muslim masses.

The schism has entirely resulted from the disagreement regarding who should be the first caliph to succeed Muhammad. Ali claimed that priority in view of a variety of factors dealt with below. It was a matter of succession, not a matter of faith, especially that both Sunnis and Shiis pay homage to the same Book, the Quran. Both factions also believe in the one-ness of God, make the same profession of faith (the Shahadah), pray towards the same Qiblah (Mecca).[129] And in fact write both Arabic and Persian by using the same alphabet.

Yet, unfortunately, the political issue of the immediate succession of the Prophet Muhammad has been conflated to create a fiction of a Sunni Islam and a Shii Islam. Evidence abounds on why this fiction has taken root. It is the conflation made by some authors of the near parallelism of personal attributes of the Prophet Muhammad and his cousin, Ali. It was the Prophet who brought Ali up. An example of this conflation is this quotation from Al-Qazweeni who states: **"God (Allah) has created Muhammad and Ali Ibn Abi-Taleb to have each of them be a perfect example on the Heavenly power, and a living testimony on the highest being in the upward scale of perfection."[130]**

Such adoring statements may be described as character references. But they did not stand in the way of Al-Qazweeni to coming down to the real reason for the Sunni-Shii split. Referring to bypassing Ali as a Caliph three times, he describes the pre-Ali Caliphates in these words: **"A quarter of a century**

---

[129] See Muhammad Hussein Haikal, <u>Life of Muhammad</u> (Cairo: Dar Al-Marrif, 2015) 25th edition (In Arabic) pp. 44-45.

[130] Al-Sayed Muhammad Kazem Al-Qazweeni, <u>Imam Ali From Cradle to Grave</u> (Beirut, Manshorat Al-Fajr, No Date). P.6 (In Arabic. Author's translation).

elapsed with Imam Ali sitting at home, deprived of power, bereft of the ability to shoulder the duties of the Caliphate... That painful period ended with the assassination of Othman (the Third Caliph, following Abu-Bakr and Omar). At that point, the Caliphate reverted to the Imam after its usurpation from him ..."[131]

From the above and from endless other evidences, it becomes clear that the Sunni-Shii split has no religious basis, but a political one. On this premise, the following narrative is based. It espouses another facet of the new Islamic religious revolution whose goals is the reunification of the broad and diverse Muslim community. Al-Azhar has been in the forefront of that battle for reunification.

We start by stating that the succession of the Prophet Muhammad did not have a set pattern. Each of the first three Caliphs was chosen in a different way. Abu-Bakr was the choice of Omar; Omar was recommended by Abu-Bakr; and Othman was chosen by **"the group of six,"** praised by Muhammad for their emigration from Mecca to Medina in defense of their faith. That was a choice made by Omar as he laid dying, a victim of an assassin.[132]

But Ali, the last of these **"enlightened caliphs,"** was the only one chosen directly by the people. The populace were in fear of mayhem resulting from Othman's assassination by Egyptian and Iraqi rebels. That controversy which plagued Othman's reign was due to various factors: He was from the Bani Ummayah, late-comers to Islam; rich and given to nepotism; and permissive in sharp contrast to his predecessor, Omar, who was both tough and austere.

Though Othman was credited with the laborious gathering of all parts of the Quran, his reign suffered from corruption throughout that new far-flung Muslim empire. Ali's counsel to Othman had little effect on Othman's ways, causing Ali frequent recusals from the seat of power in Medina. That is in spite of the fact that Ali was one of **"the group of six"** revered as Shura custodians as mentioned above. Both Othman and Ali were members of that select inner circle.[133]

---

[131] <u>Ibid</u>, p.7.

[132] Taha Hussin, op-cit., p.6.

[133] The six members of the Shura circle were: Othman, Ali, Abdel-Rahman Ibn Auf, Saad Ibn Abi Waqqas, Al-Zubeir Ibn Al-Awwam, and Talha Ibn Obaidallah.

The centrality of bypassing Ali for the Caliphate three times as the cause of divisiveness is borne out even by definitions in major Islamic dictionaries. Here is the wording in one such dictionary: **"Shia is a large sector of Muslims who are united on the belief that Ali Ibn Abi-Taleb was more entitled to the Caliphate than Abu-Bakr, and that the succession to this Caliphate should have been in Ali's sons."**[134]

The bases for the Shii belief in Ali's victimization through ignoring his claim to the immediate succession of Muhammad are abundantly documented. The vote for Abu-Bakr taking place while Ali was burying his cousin the Prophet Muhammad was especially galling. Omar orchestrated the choice of Abu-Bakr at a place called Saqifat Bani Saaidah as a way out of the emerging claim of the Ansar of Madinah to co-rulership with the Muhajeroon of Mecca. The entire conclave at Saqifat Bani Saaidah is reported to have not exceed a dozen such individuals.

Registering his dismay at being sidelined by that manoeuvre, Imam Ali said in reference to Abu-Bakr: **"Someone has assumed it (the Caliphate), though, by God, he knows that my position entitling me to it is akin to the pole holding two stones between which wheat is ground into flour."**[135]

Let us here note that Ali's claim is rooted in his being raised by Muhammad. He was the cousin of the Prophet; was brought up by Muhammad as of the age of two; was the first to adopt Islam after Khadeejah, Muhammad spouse; was the first male to pray with Muhammad; was 10 years of age when Muhammad began his mission for Islam. Add to this an iconic episode of saving the Prophet's life, thereby saving Islam itself. Ali was instructed by Muhammad to occupy his bed as a ruse allowing Muhammad to flee Mecca, together with Abu-Bakr, to Medinah. Thus Muhammad's life was saved from a hostile siege of his home by Islam's opponents. Then Ali, having returned all bailments entrusted to Muhammad by all those who had trusted the Prophet with

---

[134] Quoted from The Basic Arabic Dictionary (Al-Mojam Al-Arabi Al-Asasi), produced by ALESCO, equivalent to UNESCO, but under the aegis of the League of Arab States (Tunis, June 1988). Distributed by Larousse.

[135] Speeches by Imam Ali in <u>Nahj Al-Balaghah (The Clear Path to Eloquence)</u>; the Shaqshaqiah speech; Annotation by Imam Muhammad Abdoh (Cairo: Dar Al-Fajr Liltorath, 2005) p.68 (In Arabic).

their property joined Muhammad in Medinah where he married Fatimah, Muhammad's daughter.

Furthermore, Ali was directly involved in all combat operations led by Muhammad in a series of defensive wars against the anti-Islamic forces. He earned Muhammad's praise who, on his way to the last pilgrimage, declared: **"Whoever regarded me as his master, so with Ali. May God support whoever supports him, and punish whoever was adversarial towards him."** Abu-Bakr, Omar and Othman, as Caliphs, sought Ali's counsel which he freely gave.[136] That is despite his expressed bitterness at being bypassed for the caliphate not once, not twice, but three times.

The arguments against anointing him as the first successor of Muhammad were mainly of tribal nature. Ali was from Bani Hashem, the Prophet's lineage within the vast and economically rich tribe of Quraish, based in Mecca. It was felt that the honor of that succession should be diffused outside Bani Hashem. Though Ali, by Omar's admission,[137] was the most knowledgeable about the doctrinal intricacies of the new faith, the tribal factor prevailed.

There was also the insincere pretext about Ali's being too young to shoulder the heavy responsibilities of that awesome succession. All such arguments were regarded by those who revered Ali as phoney and counterfeit. With the choice of Othman, three successions, considered unethical by the moral standards of Ali and his sympathizers, marked a crucial change in the course of Islamic rule.

Again the reasons were tribally-based, although Islam advocated detribalization. Whereas Abu-Bakr and Omar were early and crucial supporters of the new religion, Othman was from Bani Ummayah, a tribal branch which spearheaded the struggle against Islam. That opposition continued until Mecca was reclaimed by the Muslims, sweeping by the thousands from Medina, with their swords aloft. The opposition was fearful of the Muslims avenging themselves for past injuries and grievances. But such retribution was avoided through the Prophet's magnanimity. The anti-Muslim Quraishis asked the victorious Prophet: **"What are you going to do with us?"** His response was a general pardon as he declared: **"Go!! You are pardoned (freed) (Al-Tolaqa).**

---

[136] Taha Hussein, <u>op. Cit.</u>, pp.16-17.

[137] <u>Ibid</u>, p.15.

Nearly all the Ummayads were within the category of **"the Pardoned -an epithet by tribal mores."** In tribal parlance, that was regarded as being lower than others whether Meccans or Medinans who espoused Islam out of belief, not out of defeat.

Ali and his uncle Al-Abbas have always regarded that their branch of the tribe of Quraish, namely Bani Hashem, as the first to be entitled to the succession. Their view was reinforced by the Prophet himself. While not pronouncing Ali as his successor, the Prophet's conduct and words gave out leading signals. Muhammad had called Ali **"my brother,"** and likened that relationship to the position of Aaron, to his brother Moses.[138]

On these bases, Al-Abbas, Ali's uncle, wanted to declare his fealty to Ali. Following the Bayaa for Abu-Bakr, Ali demurred as he feared divisiveness in Muslim ranks in view of Abu-Bakr installation as the First Caliph.[139]

This combination of wisdom, sacrifice, victimization by others, and readiness to serve the Muslim community, has made Imam Ali a hero for all ages. His language is Quranic; his central belief is the public good jurisdiction; his central view of the Muslim community is its one-ness; his quest is not power but justice. Wisdom (Hekmah, in Arabic) is regarded as his path to eternal salvation, and ijtihad (extrapolation of rules from occurrences on which there is no text either in the Quran or the Prophet's tradition) is his modus operandi.[140]

Ijtihad gave the Shii path to renewal. That process, among others, bestowed credibility on the adage **"Sharia is relevant to all times and places."** In all of this, there is nothing which might be regarded as in opposition to the Sunnis four schools of thought.

The central thesis of Imam Ali, of Al-Azhar in Cairo, and of thoughtful Muslim scholars, has been expressed in the dedication of Rajab Al-Banna's book in Arabic. It reads:**"To all those who believe that Islam is one faith, not amenable to divisiveness or partition; to all those who**

---

[138] Ibid, p.17.

[139] Id.

[140] Rajab Al-Banna, The Shia and Sunna: Differences in Law, Thought and History (Cairo: Dar Al-Maarif, 2004), p.160.

welcome diversity in view of its being a positive element; and to all those who believe that truth is the quest of the believer and of Islam as a faith of tolerance, not violence."[141]

The persistence of the fiction of two Islams, one Sunni (90%), the other Shii (10%) is nothing but mythology. It has been noted above that all Muslims have one holy book, the Quran; one belief in the one-ness of God; one direction towards which they pray; one recitation of the profession of faith; and one verse with which action, including prayer is begun: **"In the Name of God, the Merciful and the Compassionate."** In that context, apostasy (takfeer) is never allowed. Reason: No individual can usurp from God the power to judge humanity on Judgement Day.

The whole fictitious narrative of a Sunni Islam and a Shii Islam has, in modern times, fueled jihadism. From the inception of Al-Qaeda to ISIS, Boko Haram, and Al-Shabab of Somalia, Shiism has been regarded as apostasy. All the Emirs of death, such as Bin Laden, Zawahiri, Al-Zarqawi, and Al-Baghdadi are Sunnis. They all believed that the Shiis were **"conspiring with an outside belligerent -the United States... thus justified their slaughter."[142]**

In spite of the destruction of ISIS in both Mosul (Iraq) and Raqqah (Syria), in 2017 by an international coalition assisting local forces, one should expect the emergence of cancerous jihadi cells carrying on with that murderous ideology.

In an editorial in the **New York Times** entitled **"The Challenge After Mosul,"** the paper notes: **"The longer-term challenge will be addressing the complex factors that have created conditions for the group (ISIS) to thrive, including destructive rivalries between Sunni and Shii Muslims."[143]**

With a view to defeating jihadism by ideology, Imam Ahmed El-Taiyeb of Al-Azhar redefined the term Islam in the language of the Quran. He postulated that Islam does not stand as meaning a special faith. He declared

---

[141] Ibid, p.3.

[142] Shiraz Maher, Salafi-Jihadism: The History of an Idea (New York: Oxford University Press, 2016), p.63.

[143] The New York Times, July 12, 2017, p.A18.

it to be the word for a common universal faith, advocated by all prophets, and adhered to by all believers in those missions.[144]

The myth of a Sunni Islam and a Shii Islam has no authority in faith. It is anchored in the political/tribal contest which has erupted following the passing of the Prophet of Islam. To clothe that struggle for succession with a religious garb is to ignore historical realities and to countenance destructive sectarianism.[145]

---

[144] El-Taiyeb, Abuja, Nigeria, speech delivered in May 2016.

[145] The issues raised in this chapter shall be amplified by this author in an entire book in Arabic to be published in 2018/2019.

CHAPTER 12

Destroying Dictatorship as an Islamic Duty

Eleven centuries before the publication of **"The Social Contract"** by Jean Jacque Rousseau (1712-1778), Islam advocated against dictatorship. The essence of the Islamic ethos and of The Social Contract was that legitimacy in governance springs from justice for the ruled by the ruler. This may sound odd as regarding the Muslim-majority countries where the normal is one-man rule. But we are dealing here with the Islamic premise motivating the new Islamic religious revolution following the eruption of the Arab Spring as of December 2010.

One important resource on this topic is **"Islam and the Arab Awakening,"** by Tariq Ramadan. Ramadan's conclusions include the following assessment: **"The world has changed. The Arab world and Muslim majority societies not only need political uprisings; they need a thoroughgoing intellectual revolution that will open the door to economic change, and to spiritual, religious, cultural, and artistic liberation -and to the empowerment of women. What is needed is a global approach."**[146]

It is instructive to note the last paragraph in that seminal book by Ramadan. In part, it reads as follows: **"It is now essential to turn inward, to engage in self-criticism, to know our strengths and weaknesses, to yield nothing to doubt and to offer everything to hope. Beyond the question of East and West lie freedom, autonomy, courage and**

---

[146] Tariq Ramadan, <u>Islam and the Arab Awakening</u> (New York: Oxford University Press, 2012), p.142.

determination."[147]

"Freedom and autonomy" referred to above, are spelt out as anti-dictatorship precepts in a document dated August 17, 2011 entitled **"Al-Azhar Document on Egypt's Future."** That document, the product of a unique consensus among leaders of various fields, especially those aspiring to the Egyptian presidency, stipulated guidelines for constitutional formulation.

Framing the ideology of what became, as of 2014, the new Islamic religious revolution, it emphasized in its first article that **"Islam, in its legislation, civilization, and history does not recognize a religiously-based State."** Furthermore, it encapsulated the modern formulation of the Islamic precepts of Shura (popular consultation). Those precepts guarantee **"diversity, the peaceful transfer of powers, a well-defined exercise of authority, whose custodians are accountable to the people's representatives."**

Another principle in that document containing 11 principles, provided for **"commitment to basic rights and freedoms with regard to thought and opinion."**[148] Differentiating between the freedom of thought and the freedom of opinion (expression), Gamal Al-Banna, in his book in Arabic entitled **"Freedom"** (Al-Horriyah) states: **"The first is personal to the individual... The other is publicly pronounced through writing, the press, broadcasting, and conferences."**[149]

That dictatorship is anathema to Islam draws upon a multitude of Quranic verses, Muhammad's tradition, the practices of the Four Enlightened Caliphs succeeding the Prophet in leading the Muslim community, and the great reformers especially those who presided over Al-Azhar in modern times.

Looking upon dictatorship as injustice (zolm), the Quran justifies resistance to that usurpation of people's right to personal and communal freedoms.

---

[147] Ibid., p.144.

[148] Al-Azhar Document on Egypt's Future, first three principles, Cairo, August 17, 2011.

[149] Gamal Al-Banna. Freedom (Al-Horriyah) (Cairo: Dar Al-Fikr Al-Arabi, 2000), p.10 (In Arabic)

Among its dozens of verses opposing injustice, is the following: **"Permission to fight back is given to those who have been oppressed, and surely God is Most Powerful to bring their victory."**[150] From that and other similar Quranic verses, one could see that opposing dictatorship by various means, including by the force of arms, is sanctioned as self-defense.

While God in the Quran is called **"The Just,"** the Quran imposes on all the duty to act fairly. That principle of equality before the law is the substance of the following verse: **"We do not burden any soul with more than it can bear, and when you speak, be just, even if it is about one near of kin."**[151]

The definiteness in Islamic jurisprudence of the obligation imposed on Muslim communities to oust a dictatorship has to do with the concept of direct relationship between the individual and the Creator. That relationship is reflected in several ways of which the primary is Tawheed -the One-ness of God. It precludes the fealty to another human being beyond the observance of law and order. The phrase **"Allahu Akbar"** (God Is Greater) conveys the same commitment to distancing from idols, whether humans in the form of dictators, or inanimate in the form of man-made idols.

There is added emphasis on the downgrading of dictatorship as a governing system. That emphasis is made through the concept of victory for a just struggle. The Quran states: **"If God helps you, no power can overcome you. And if He forsakes you, who is there who can help you after Him?"**[152] And in another Chapter, the Quran returns to the same theme of auto-determination for the sake of freedom from tyranny. It says: **"And God made it but a message of hope, and an assurance for your hearts. And victory comes only from God. Surely God is Almighty, All-Wise."**[153]

The entire episode of the victory of Moses as a Messenger of God, over pharaoh as a human potentate, adds cogency to the obligation to struggle

---

[150] The Quran, Chapter 22, Verse 39.

[151] Ibid., Chapter 6, Verse 152.

[152] Ibid, Chapter 3, Verse 160.

[153] Ibid, Chapter 8, Verse 10.

against oppression. In a chapter entitled The Narratives (Al-Qasas), the Quran says of Pharaoh: **"We relate to you from the tidings of Moses and Pharaoh in Truth, for people who believe. Surely Pharaoh elated himself in the land and divided its people into sections, one of which he oppressed, killing their sons and sparing their women. Indeed he was a corrupter."**[154]

Now for a comparison between the styles of governance in the first stage of Islamic rule. One from the first Caliph (Abu-Bakr), the other from the Abbasid period, two periods separated by a mere two-hundred years. Upon the selection of Abu-Bakr as the first successor of the Prophet Muhammad, his first declaration was: **"I have been appointed as your leader, though I am not the best amongst you. If I do well, support me. But if I do ill, remove me."**[155]

This was a public invitation to impeach Abu-Bakr, issued at the dawn of the post-Muhammad age. A period of Islamic democracy based on public consultation (Shura), dating from the 7th century, A.D. But nearly a mere two decades, Islamic polity had experienced a drastic move from a republican mode to a monarchical mode.

The monarchical mode arose in imitation of Byzantine rule in Syria, and of Persian rule in Persia. The Abbasid, having shifted the capital of the so-called Caliphate from Damascus to Baghdad, copied the monarchical way by which that area, covering both Iraq and Iran, was ruled.

Reflecting the spirit of the divine right of monarchs, Al-Mansour Al-Abbadi declared to his Muslim subjects: **"I am the Sultan appointed by God to rule in God's lands. With His divine guidance and support, I shall manage your affairs."**[156] The pendulum of rule has swung sharply away from government by the people, to government by the kings -Muslim kings, Muslim dictators.

Yet the change in form, for whatever length of time it takes, does not alter the premise of Islamic rule as based on the Quran, the Prophet's tradition

---

[154] Ibid, Chapter 28, Verses 3 and 4.

[155] Muhammad Hussein Haykal, Life of Muhammad (Cairo: Dar Al-Maarif, 2015), 25th edition, p.63.

[156] Ibid., p.64.

and ijtihad: an unjust ruler is to be removed by his subjects. Omar, the Second Caliph and empire-builder through law and justice had laid down that solid foundation. His **"judicial proclamation,"** originally inspired by Imam Ali as his advisor, demanded evidence for an indictment. It also called for a court protocol emphasizing equality before the law. Its central feature is **"on the bench, the judge's face should reflect equality. No smile for the powerful, no consternation for the powerless."**

An entire book in Arabic on Omar, as a champion of justice by the people and for the people, was authored in the early 1930s by the great Egyptian philosopher, Abbas Mahmoud Al-Aaqqad. Its title is **"The Genius of Omar."** One of its memorable utterances by Omar is **"Since when have you enslaved people who were born by their mothers to be free?"** That was in the context of Omar exacting punishment of a son of Egypt's governor, Amre Ibn El-As who had led the Arab invasion of Egypt in the 7th century. The erring son had flogged a Coptic lad who had bested him in a game of races. Upon complaint by the Coptic father to Caliph Omar, he ordered that the governor and his son come to Medina, the capital, for that public dressing down.[157]

After Muhammad, it was Omar who was the gold standard for legislation for equality for all before the law. Thus Muslim jurists called him **"the main authority in legislation."** (For a full translation of Omar's instructions to the judiciary, see the Annexes to this book). An apt description because Omar relied not only on the Quran and the Prophet's tradition (the Hadith), but also on what is known as **"the jurisdiction of public interest."** A form of ijtihad (common sense interpretation) where there exists no textual provisions in either the Quran or the Hadith.[158]

That is why Haykal, in his book **"Life of Muhammad,"** points up the great decline in the standard of the Rule of Law within only 200 years from Islam's inception. Muslim rule in Medina, the first Islamic capital since Muhammad's days, and Muslim rule thereafter in Damascus (the Ummayads), then in Baghdad (the Abbasids) were two opposite genres. In Medina, Muslim polity was republican; away from Medina, it became oppressive monarchical hereditary. In one word: **"corruption"** (in Arabic -

---

[157] Abbas Mahmoud Al-Aaqqad, <u>The Genious of Omar</u> (Cairo: Dar Al-Maarif, No date), In Arabic.

[158] Ahmed Amin. <u>Dawn of Islam</u> (Beirut: Dar Al-Kotob Al-ilmiyah, 2009), Third Edition, p.228.

Fasad).

The exit from republicanism and into dictatorship is an abhorrent journey pointedly condemned by the Quran -the primary source of Islamic jurisdiction. (For a depiction in Arabic poetry of the hallucination by dictators about their indispensability, see the Annexes in this volume for my translation of a memorable poem by the Syrian poet, Nizar Qabbani).

A Quranic chapter deals with the Queen of Sheba, who, while in consultation with her aides regarding a message from (King) Soloman, ascribed corruption to monarchs. **"She said 'surely, kings, when they enter a town, ruin it, and make the noblest of its people abased, and thus do they behave."**[159]

In its condemnation of corruption (fasad), Quranic scripture regards extrajudicial killing, a feature of dictatorship, as evidence of corruption. **"We prescribed to the children of Israel that whoever kills a soul, unless it be for retaliation or because of spreading corruption on earth, it would be as if he had killed all mankind."**[160] Applying that threshold to jihadism, Islamic law regards the world-wide criminality of terror organizations of all stripes as having annihilated all mankind many times over.

In American courts, the sign behind the judge's bench proclaims **"In God We Trust."** So with courts of the Muslim world where the equivalent of **"In God We Trust"** read **"Judge With Justice."** This is an abbreviation of a Quranic verse which reads: **"God Commands you to render back trusts to whom they belong, and when you judge between people, that you judge with justice."**[161]

These principles, now fully endorsed by the new Islamic religious revolution as led by Al-Azhar, have found their rightful place in the post-Arab Spring constitutions, especially those of Tunisia and Egypt. Article One of the secular Egyptian Constitution of 2014, which massively amended the Islamist Constitution of 2012, deals with the State as follows: **"The Arab Republic of Egypt is a State endowed with sovereignty as**

---

[159] The Quran, Chapter 27, Verse 34.

[160] Ibid., Chapter 5, Verse 32.

[161] Ibid., Chapter 4, Verse 58.

a unitary State not subject to partition or territorial surrender, with a republican and democratic system, based on the principles of citizenship and the supremacy of the rule of law."[162]

Article 101 of the same Constitution provides for the House of Representatives (450 members chosen by secret ballot by Egyptian voters by secret ballot) charges that branch of government with legislation and oversight over the executive branch. A member of that House is inducted upon taking the oath of office by which he or she pledges **"respect for the Constitution and the law in full observance of public interest"** (Article 104).

The judicial branch's independence is provided for in Articles 184, 185 and 186. This is while the Supreme Constitutional Court, under Article 192, is tasked, among other things, with review of the constitutionality of laws and regulations and the resolution of conflicts of law. (Articles 191 and 192).

The above-referenced constitutional provisions are examples of the intertwining between Islamic law (Sharia) as based on the Quran, the Hadith, and Ijtihad, and secular legislation as supplementation. Hence it is an error, resulting from ignorance of that structure, to understand Sharia in the way that jihadists portray it. Sharia constantly evolves not only by ijtihad, but also by its supplementation by legislation.

The premise of the eclectic nature of sharia, especially in respect to fighting dictatorship of which jihadism is a manifestation, could also be found in Al-Azhar document of August 2011. It referred to **"the turbulence (in Egypt) of the Revolution of January 25, 2011 as an uprising"** which swept aside the military rule of 60 years. Nasser of Egypt, who had engineered that rule in July 1952, was nothing but a dictator.

The same Al-Azhar document also stated in the 3rd of its 11 principles the following: **"Commitment to basic rights and freedoms with regard to both thought and opinion, including full respect of the rights of the individual, of women and children, and of the principles of diversity. Citizenship is the primary basis from which emanates obligations to society."**

The religious obligation on Muslims to remove dictatorship is conditioned

---

[162] The Constitution of the Arab Republic of Egypt, promulgated on January 18, 2014, Article I.

only by the ability of a community to overcome a dictatorial rule without incurring a total breakdown of law and order. Such a breakdown is what is generally termed in Islamic jurisprudence as mayhem, insurrection, otherwise known by its Quranic term as **"Fitna."** The Quran states: **"And fear tumult of oppression, which affects not in particular only those of you who do wrong. And know that Allah is strict in punishment."** [163] Hence that obligation is conditioned on averting a resultant insurrection.

In a speech before the Conference of Muslim Wisemen (Hukama Al-Muslimoon) held in Cairo in 2016, Al-Azhar's Grand Imam, Dr. Ahmed El-Taiyeb termed the right to freedom from coercion as an inalienable right. Within the scope of that freedom, he squarely placed the freedoms of religion, of belief, and of adherence to any school of religious thought (Mazhab). Bestowing on those freedoms a Quranic sanction, he cited: **"There is no compulsion in Religion."**[164]

It is therefore logical to conclude that within the Islamic religious revolution, the concept of freedom from oppression, for reasons of faith or governance, entails also the right to resist. As an inherent right, it cannot be given away by any human who possesses it since birth as stressed by Omar, the Second Caliph.

As early in the Arab Spring as November 2011, Dr. El-Taiyeb, at a press conference in Cairo, expounded upon the Muslim's duty to resists dictatorship. Referring to the uprisings in Tunisia, Egypt, and Libya against their respective dictators, the Grand Imam of Al-Azhar declared: **"The legitimacy of any governance is contingent upon the popular will. The right to peaceful opposition is guaranteed by Islamic legislation. This is due to the principle of that legislation calling for extinguishing harm to the populace. This is in addition to the provisions in international conventions regarding such resistance as integral to human rights.**

The struggle for the rule of law has been a non-ending struggle for the entire recorded history of humanity. Islamophobes have mis-characterized that struggle in the Muslim world as natural only for Muslim societies. They are wrong as they cannot convincingly explain the following phenomena: The rise of Nazism and fascism in Europe of the 20th century; the imperial

---

[163] The Quran, Chapter 8, Verse 25.

[164] Ibid., Chapter 2, Verse 256.

nature of governance in Japan before World War II; the grip of monolithic communism in Europe and Asia. The fact of the matter is that religion does not produce dictatorships. But dictatorships produce in Muslim societies phony religious pretexts. In this regard, dictatorships and jihadism parallel one another.

CHAPTER 13

Wahhabism: A Reform Degenerated Into A Theocracy

In the geographic center of the Arabian peninsula, (Diriyah, Najd) arose an Islamic reformer, Muhammad Ibn Abdel-Wahhab (1703-1787). Imbued by the need to return Islam to its original simplicity, though within a stricter framework. He called for doing away with ceremonialism, fetishes, like ornate tombs and ritual visitations, and for female modesty in dress and appearance. His thesis in Tawheed (the one-ness of God) was the veneration of the Quran and the adherence to the example of the Prophet Muhammad, (sunna). No call for jihad in that advocacy, and no oppression of women.

The heart of that reformist Wahhabism was that **"reform should be a process, beginning at the grassroots level and moving gradually upward through society as people's private ethical and moral beliefs, grounded in their religion, influenced decision making and public conduct."**[165] None of these advocacies for reform was either revolutionary, backward looking, or even an implication of the force of arms as a means for the protection or the spread of Islam. Not even a hint of jihadism.

Such was the spirit of the 18th century Wahhabism, that it was natural for Sheikh Muhammad Abdoh, the great Egyptian Islamic reformer (1849-1905) to fully endorse Wahhabism. After all, the book on Tawheed by Ibn Abdel-Wahhab and that on the same topic by Abdoh read nearly alike.

---

[165] Natana J. Delong-Bas, <u>Wahhabi Islam: From Revival and Reform to Global Jihad</u> (New York City: Oxford University Press, 2009), p.9.

On the critical issue of jihad, neither Ibn Abdel-Wahhab, nor Abdoh called on Muslims to initiate aggressive warfare on non-Muslim countries. As shall be seen in subsequent chapters, there is no holy war in Islam -a thesis which is central tenet in the new Islamic religious revolution. Self-defense, yes; aggression, as waged by jihadists inspired by the degeneration of the original wahhabism, no.

The degeneration of Wahhabism from a reform movement in the 19th century to a theocracy in the 20th century is mainly due to the compact reached by King Abdel-Aziz Al Saud with Al Alsheikh, the descendants of Ibn Abdel-Wahhab. That compact had the effect of co-governance between the Saudis and Al-Alsheikh. The former would rule the Kingdom, now united by the Saudi sword; the latter would have a free reign in dictating to the populace what Islam meant.

The result was the emergence of a theocracy that, until today, does not reflect the enlightened face of the original wahhabism. Spirituality became a set of rituals and practices. Above all, it did not recognize **"the other"** who differed in faith, nor the freedom of expression and belief, nor the right to the openness of society to art, music, dance, theater and the like. Nor does it see women as equal to men in transactions, autodetermination, equal treatment in employment, or the ability to share equally in the broad life of society.

The theocratic side of Saudi governance manifests itself in various ways which have retarded the progress of Saudi Arabia toward becoming an industrial society. How could it: Employment of women is restricted to nursing, teaching and limited social work; an embargo of males and females working together; enforced closure of stores, offices, and restaurants, when the call to prayer sounds (observant Muslims pray five times a day); the black abayas (long loose dress) cover women from head to toe, plus a hijab or a niqab (from which only slits are made to allow the eyes to see).

In addition to these features imposed by the cultish wahhabism, women are prevented to drive cars; they cannot travel alone except in the company of a male who is a blood relation to the female; music and other forms of arts and artistic expression are forbidden; a woman attorney cannot plead a case in a court of law unless accompanied or represented by a male attorney; and religious police (so-called volunteers) roam the streets of the kingdom at will armed with sticks to enforce these non-faith-based practices.

The Ministry of Justice is in the hands of Al Elsheikh; the Council of the Grand Ulamas (scholars) are the fount of advisory opinions flowing from this Wahhabi understanding of Islam; there is no constitution except for rules extrapolated by these cave-minded but exalted persons as Islamic. And the Quran itself, and most of the Hadith (Muhammad's tradition) are the only bases for adjudication in a court of law, or for fatwas (religious opinions), as means for the enhancement of law and order in society. Most legislation (man-made law) is suspect.

Theocratic Wahhabism in Saudi society and abroad has been propagated by a restricted educational system throughout its various stages. And parallel systems have been generously funded by the vast Saudi petro-wealth through Madrasas (schools) established in Asia, Africa, and Saudi roving missions in other parts of the world. Thus the openness of Islam to evolution through common sense and the application of Hekmah (Wisdom) has been nullified. I once attended in Riyadh in 1983 a mass Friday prayer where the preacher assured the congregation that **"paradise consists of actual houses filled with all kinds of amenities. He was the Dean of a Saudi college."**

Calling itself **"sunni,"** is a Wahhabi abuse of the term whose original meaning is to follow in the steps of the Prophet Muhammad, through, among other things, the observance of changing circumstances and the freedom of **"the other."** One cannot see **"sunnism"** in the Saudi practice of public flogging, or beheading; in the spread of the notion that jihad, through aggressive armed confrontations anywhere and everywhere, is a duty incumbent upon every Muslim to pursue; and that the only Islam recognizable by Wahhabism is Sunni Islam. Shiism is made an apostasy to be eliminated. It is no surprise that rebellion among the Shiis who inhabit the eastern part of the kingdom has been a frequent challenge to the Government.

The consequences of wahhabism regionally and globally have been devastating. For wahhabism exalted jihadism to the point that 15 out of 19 perpetrators of the crime of 9/11 in the US hailed from Saudi Arabia.[166] Funding of this cultism has subverted moderate Islam in southeast Asia, especially in Pakistan, Malaysia and Indonesia. The terrorist wing of the Muslim Brotherhood in Egypt ended by taking over that entire movement, resulting in its rejection by the vast majority in that State of nearly 100 million Arabs. Various national laws and international agreements countering terrorism had little effect in restraining the spread of jihadism.

---

[166] Ibid., p.193.

Though Saudi Arabia itself has suffered from the boomerang of that jihadism, it dealt with the problem on two levels. Internal incidents are regarded as terrorism, such as in the case of the assassination attempts on the life of Prince Muhammad Bin Nayef, the former Interior Minister. But external events are met with either silence or with pro forma condemnation. The primary difference between the teaching of Ibn Abdel-Wahhab and today's wahhabism is that the founder called for knowledge of the Quran and the Hadith at the mass level, whereas the latter considered that knowledge was the preserve of the select few.[167] Theocracy is the consequence of the latter as it creates a governance by immediately presumed divine guidance. Such is the form, context, and substance of today's wahhabism.

The cumulative effect is to discern the gaping distance between obscurant wahhabism and the advocacy of today's new Islamic religious revolution. One, wahhabism of today, is an inspiration to violence. (Bin Laden did not happen from a vacuum). The other, is reflected in what Al-Azhar is preaching on the basis of both scriptures and evolved practices.

The Quran is diametrically opposed to the wahhabi narrative. It advises as follows: **"There is no compulsion in Religion."**[168] And **"The Trust is from your Lord. Let him who will believe, and let him who will reject it."**[169] Yet, the wahhabi religious police in Jeddah, finding a car driver sitting in his car at the time of prayer, felt that it was his sacred duty to force him out of his car to perform that ritual. That is even after he pleaded with them that he had not performed ablution, a pre-prayer act of purification by water before prayers.[170]

In his speech in Abuja, Nigeria, in May 2016, the Grand Imam of Al-Azhar cited these Quranic verses to bolster his argument: **"Relation between persons of different views and beliefs is aligned with the nature of differences. It is illogical and unwise to think that God has ordained these differences then goes back to instruct that they should be forced to do what they, by their own disposition, do not wish to do."**

---

[167] <u>Ibid</u>., pp.194-195.

[168] The Quran, Chapter 2, Verse 256.

[169] <u>Ibid</u>., Chapter 18, Verse 29.

[170] Anecdotal, in an interview with a Jaddah resident.

Then he goes on to defeat the Wahhabi thesis in regard to fighting non-Muslims for being **"non-believers."** These are his words: **"It is incorrect and is very regrettable to believe that fighting for the sake of Islam is a legitimate pursuit because of the others being non-Muslims. This is pure fabrication of Islam and of Muhammad's tradition. In Islam, combat is made just, only in cases of aggression and of repelling suppression."**

These Azhari views were earlier expounded in 2011 following the Egyptian Revolution of January 2011 in the famous document of August of that year under the title of **"A Declaration by Al-Azhar and the Intellectual Community on the System of Basic Freedoms."**[171]

It is truly tragic that Wahhabism, in its present theocratic phase, has fallen from the thought summit of its founder to today's abyss. Its ideological phase of purifying Islam from cultism was its past. Its present is nothing but a retrograde cult. While Saudi Arabia's wahhabi co-rulers refuse the admission of the importation of the bible into their country, it felt offended when the US, in reciprocity, stopped the importation in bulk of copies of the Quran into America.

It therefore seems tragically comic that the Organization of Islamic Cooperation (OIC), consisting of 57 States of Muslim majorities, has its headquarters in Jeddah, Saudi Arabia; that the fiction of Shiis being **"rejectionists"** has been elevated to a geostrategic level of a sunni alliance in the Gulf against Iran; that the war in Yemen between the Houthis (a branch of Shiism) and the Saudi-backed Yemeni Government of Abdu-Rabboh is propagated as a struggle for containment of an Iranian attempt for influence expansion; and that the Iranian nuclear deal reached in 2016 between Iran and all members of the UN Security Council, plus Germany, is a destabilizing factor.

Tribalism in the Wahhabi practices cannot be underestimated. The impact of this ingrained tribalism has accelerated it into becoming a cult. This is especially so in the realms of women, society and jihad. A meeting with the Council of the Grand Ulemas (scholars) in Riyadh in the 2004 showed me the depth of this Wahhabi predicament. At that meeting, while expecting a broadly-based discussion regarding the role of Islam in modern society, the

---

[171] Documents by Al-Azhar Al-Shareef (Cairo: Al-Azhar Press, November 2011). Document No.3. In Arabic.

group was interested only in one topic. Their questioning me revolved around one inquiry: **"Brother Yassin: Do you read the Quran?"**

I left that meeting empty-handed, lamenting the departure of present-day Wahhabism from its original anchor in the thought of that reformer, Muhammad Ibn Abdel-Wahhab. The following passage is a measure of that departure. **"Ibn Abd Al-Wahhab's emphasis on the importance of Islamic values and the intent behind these words and actions, as opposed to concern for ritual perfection, has opened the door for reforms in Islamic law, the status of women and minorities and the peaceful spread of Islam and the Islamic mission in the contemporary era."[172]**

The reformist founder of Wahhabism called for ijtihad, the practice of independent reasoning, and for **"a break away from a mentality insisting that only people who had lived in the past were capable of correct interpretation of scripture."[173]** (i.e. The Quran and Muhammad's tradition -sunna). This constituted an ideological rejection of **Salafism** (the movement of imitating those who espoused Islam at its early stages). It is well-known, at least from the experience of Egypt with the wayward Muslim Brotherhood from 2011 to 2013 and beyond, that Salafism is the Brotherhood but with a different name. An enforced veneration of the religiosity of the past without regard to the changing of circumstances, nor to the good examples established by the Prophet Muhammad himself.

In this regard, the Prophet Muhammad has pointedly called for freedom of religious choices and rejected any attempt to enforced abdication of Judaism, Christianity or any other form of faith. Dr. El-Taiyeb has quoted this on point Mohammedan Hadith: **"If a Jew or a Christian abhors Islam in favor of his faith, no one can compel him to change course."[174]**

So if present day Wahhabism is propagandizing the adherence to scriptures (the Quran and the Hadith), it is merely reflecting a clear misinterpretation of both, leading to the present crisis of near global fear of Islam as a faith of the sword, out of tune with the times, and should be regarded as a threat to

---

[172] Delong-Bas, op. Cit., p. 281.

[173] Ibid., p. 282.

[174] Dr. El-Taiyeb's speech in Abuja, Nigeria, May 2016.

international peace and security.

An article in the **New York Times Magazine** of July 30, 2017, entitled **"Guilt Free,"** quoted Jeff Sieting, president of a village in Michigan in his Facebook page. He calls for **"the United States to kill every last Muslim, and declares that Islam a flesh-eating bacteria."**

This is beyond the redlines of Islamophobia, and is couched in Sieting retort: **"I owe nobody an apology for exercising my First Amendment rights."**[175] Another facet of that person's ignorance of what is **"a protected speech"** which puts his advocacy beyond the protection of the First Amendment of the US Constitution for its being a call to violence.

In such climate, various attempts by US President Donald Trump to ban the entry into the U.S. of nationals of several Muslim majority countries have been made. Though such attempts have faced judicial challenges by federal courts for being unconstitutional, they revealed the depth of concern for national security from arrivals who happen to be Muslims.

The Wahhabism of today, because of its cultish departure from its reformist foundations, its rejection of **"the other,"** its advocacy of jihad through its Madrassas in Saudi Arabia and abroad, and its theocratic dominance in that Kingdom, is the reason why the new Islamic Religious revolution looks upon it as inimical to what Islam and Islamic law are all about.

---

[175] Wesley Morris, "Guilt Free," in <u>The New York Times Magazine</u>, July 30, 2017, p.11.

CHAPTER 14

The Quranic Term 'Read' Means 'Learn'

"Iqra," meaning **"Read"** is the first word of the Quran. It also has a broader meaning - **"learn."** In Islam, learning, in the sense of acquiring knowledge or experience, has no bounds. All disciplines, subjects, and learnable experiences are not separated from one another. Thus it could be said that a Muslim scholar (Alem -the plural of which is Ulama) is essentially an encyclopedic learner. History, geography, math, and physics are no more than various facets of knowledge, with no compartmentalization.

In Islamic tradition, the basis of this approach to learning could be found in the Quran. **"Can those be equal: they who know and they who know not."**[176]

"The Book" being the Quran, and the **"Hekmah"** (Wisdom), bring the application of reason to matters on which there is no scripture: This is the essence of the Non-Textual Islamic Jurisdiction. It is the fount of ijtihad (see the following chapter). Thus **"Hekmah"** is the primary gap-filler of scripture, allowing for knowledge by interpretation or extrapolation (Extrapolation being the calculation from known terms other terms) to be taken into account. This is how man-made or man-thought knowledge is created. A mechanism for continual knowledge expansion and diversification.

The importance of this process lies in its keeping Sharia evolving constantly

---

[176] The Quran, Chapter 39, Verse 9.

in the light of changing circumstances. This makes for the rejuvenation of belief, making it keep pace with changing conditions and environments unforeseen at the dawn of Islam. This is the essence of the Islamic adage **"Sharia is suitable everywhere and for all time."** Unfortunately, this adage has been misinterpreted by both jihadists and Islamphobes as a call for the forcefull imposition of Sharia on non-Muslim societies.

From the dawn of Islam, this religious movement was driven by three sources: **"The Quran and its interpretation; the Hadith and its collection and listing by subject matter; and the extrapolation of rules from events and occurrences which we call jurisdiction."**[177]

As noted above, the word **"Quran"** itself means a book of readings. With Arabia itself where it was revealed, being parched desert, with little learning except for poetry and pre-Islamic idolatry being considered as knowledge, it became incumbent upon Islam's adherents to borrow from their neighbors. To the south was a vibrant Yemeni Jewish civilization; to the east was the rich Zoroastrianism culture of Persia; to the north was Byzantium, the home of Christian orthodoxy. Thus from early times, the Muslims realized that knowledge is power. The quest for it became a mission.

Al-Madinah, the capital of the first Islamic State, was called Yathrib -a Jewish colony. It consisted of Jewish immigrants to Arabia, and Arabs who became Jews. Motivating this process of immigration and conversion was Christian Byzantine oppression of the Jews of the north (Syria of old). Among those were the tribes of Banu Nudair, Banu Quraizah, and Banu Bahdal. All experts in the industries of blacksmithing, agriculture, and arms-making.[178]

The Arab tribe of Quraish, from which Muhammad hailed, became rich and famous in pre-Islamic times because of trade. The Quran speaks of the annual trading trips of winter and summer. **"For the tradition of Quraish. Their tradition of traveling in winter and summer."**[179] The word **"Quraish"** refers to **"Qirsh,"** a coin. That was indicative of Quraish being a kind of **"the Chicago Products Exchange,"** or a little and early Wall

---

[177] Ahmed Amin, <u>The Dawn of Islam</u> (Fajr Al-Islam), (Beirut: Dar Al-Kotob Al-ilmiyah, 1971); p.189. (In Arabic)

[178] <u>Ibid</u>, p.34.

[179] <u>The Quran</u>, Chapter 106, Verses 1 and 2.

Street. Before Islam, Muhammad was a trader -an honest trader who earned the name of **"Muhammad Al-Amin"** (Muhammad the Honest). A description later befitting a prophet.

The seepage from one culture into another was manifest in Alexandria, Egypt -a country where monotheism was born at the hands of Ikhnaton - the father of King Tut. There the thought of Rome, Greece and Syria became one amalgam of civilizations, science and faith.

So the search for knowledge by the Arabs, in the pre-Islamic period and the post-Islamic, had a strong impetus from all these influences. Bolstering that quest for knowledge was the Prophet Muhammad's Hadith: **"Search for knowledge, even in China."** That was a call from Muhammad who, as regards reading and writing, was described as **"the illiterate Prophet"** (Al-Nabi Al-Ummyy).

The Quran was obviously the primary influencer for that ceaseless actualizing of the word (Iqra) (learn). The eclecticism of that learning was not only geographically and commercially motivated. It also had a religious orientation in that Islam as a faith equated respect for humanity with respect for all things created by God -animate and inanimate. On this point, we have the words of the Grand Imam of Al-Azhar, Sheikh Ahmed El-Taiyeb.

Here follow samples of his declarations: **"It should be asserted without doubt, to both the adherents and non-adherents of Islam that Islam is a faith of peace. I do not say 'peace only to human beings,' but also to the entire universe, including animals, plants and inanimate objects."**[180]

In these declarations, we find clear rebuff by the new Islamic religious revolution to jihadism which has ferociously engaged in the wanton destruction of the great cultural heritages of Syria, Iraq, and other locations. For they look upon these icons, not as national IDs and civilizational repositories. But as **"idols"** that do not fit within their concept of Islamic faith and culture. This destructive tendency by jihadism was even reflected in the Muslim Brotherhood's outlook upon ancient Egyptian monuments as **"unislamic."** The only cultural heritage respected by those cultural thugs is the use of the sword and of the wrecking ball in Mosul (Iraq) and Raqqah (Syria).

---

[180] El-Taiyeb's Speech in Abuja, Nigeria, May 2016.

Great Islamic reformers like Sheikh Muhammad Abdoh warned against that cultural genocide, as early as the 19th century. He has famously proclaimed: **"Islam was an Arab Faith, which latched itself to science, thus becoming an Arab science."**[181]

The linkage between Islam and learning is made clear by Muhammad Hussein Heykal in his book on the life of Muhammad referred to above. He provides multiple evidences that: **"God has decreed in his Book that the logic of the human mind is the crown of this human life. This is providing that that logic has to be integrative logic. Such logic has to conciliate itself with the mind, the passion and the spirit. This is the only way that humanity can fathom the secrets of the universe."**[182]

The linkage between learning (knowledge), wisdom (hekmah), and faith is asserted by several verses in the Quran. In fact, **"The Book"** delves deeper in order to anchor that linkage. Thus it goes back to the roots of Islam as it invokes the age of Solomon and David. **"To Solomon, We inspired the right understanding of the matter: to each of them We gave judgment and knowledge."**[183]

Commenting on that verse, the late Grand Imam of Al-Azhar, Dr. Muhammad Sayed Tantawi says: **"We (reference to God's words) have bestowed on these two prophets the gifts of prophethood, and the cogency of words and deeds. In addition, (We) have provided both of them with an understanding of jurisprudence. That is to say that correct comprehension of subject indeed matters."**[184]

Reference was made above to the encyclopedic nature of Islamic learning. That characteristic is manifest not only in subject matters. It also has deep roots in various cultures. Although these were religious cultures, their impact was readily felt in the modes of secular thought and governance.

---

[181] As quoted in Muhammad Hussein Heykal, <u>Life of Muhammad</u> (Cairo: Dar Al-Maaref, 2015), 25th edition, p.450. (In Arabic).

[182] <u>Ibid</u>, p.448.

[183] <u>The Quran</u>, Chapter 21, Verse 79.

[184] Dr. Muhammad Sayed Tantawi, <u>The Art of Dialogue in Islam -Selections</u>, (Cairo: The Egyptian Ministry of Culture and Education, 2014-2015), p.33.

Judaism and Christianity being present in Arabia before Islam, the two older religions had the greatest share of impacting Islamic search for knowledge. Persia and India and Greece and Rome were a part of that mix, especially in the realms of philosophy, translation, geography, law, and physical sciences.[185]

Bearing in mind that Arabic culture and education have two sides, one religious, the other linguistic, both influenced by other cultural non-Arab feeders, we find confirmation of this multifaceted phenomenon in main statements voiced by the Grand Imam of Al-Azhar. In his speech before the European Parliament in 2016, Dr. El-Taiyeb said: **"It has been both natural and logical that Islam has been open, in a meaningful way, to the effects of Christians and Jews. Thus Islam has extended to them and others bridges of coexistence and mutual peace. Such features have made it possible for a Muslim male to marry a Christian or Jewish female, with the non-Muslim spouse keeping the practices of her faith."[186]**

Shifting his narrative to the impact of such multifaceted knowledge to its relevance to the war on jihadism, the Grand Imam of Al-Azhar went on to say: **"Democracy, which we now aspire to its spread far and wide in our Arab and Muslim countries, cannot be realized by wars, cultural conflicts, chaos said to be 'constructive,' blood letting and saber rattling. Democracy can only be spread by inter-civilizational exchanges between you and us, a dialogue between equals, free from being oppressive, and exchange programs in the fields of education, science, and technology."[187]**

These precepts are integral parts of the new Islamic religious revolution which Al-Azhar has spearheaded. Looking back into the history of Al-Azhar's espousal of these anti-jihadi thoughts, one should take it to the anti-colonial struggle in Egypt waged as of the end of the 19th century. With Jamal El-Din Afghani and Muhammad Abdoh (both Islamic

---

[185] Ahmed Amin, <u>Islam's Mid-Morning</u> (Dhoha Al-Islam) (Cairo, Maktabet El-Nahda Al-Misriyah, 1961) Vol. One, pp.373-408. (In Arabic)

[186] El-Taiyeb, Speech Before the European Parliament, Berlin, on March 15, 2016

[187] <u>Id</u>.

reformers, the former from Iran, the latter from Egypt), the religious reform movement took on an anti-colonial decisive turn. Operating partly in Egypt, then in France, then in Turkey, that advocacy eventually ignited the 1919 Egyptian rebellion against British occupation. Learning, religion, and political resistance to occupation became one issue, though of various facets.

With the decline of educational levels in the Arab/Muslim worlds, a decline to which dictatorships have been a primary contributor, religiosity and misinterpretation of Islam and Sharia became an industry. The yen for renewal of knowledge and for cultural enrichment through international exchanges diminished. In such darkening environments, the mold of jihadism as a means to regaining past strength grew thicker.

The main casualty of such obscurantism was the enlightened practice of accepting **"the other"** as a modicum of peaceful coexistence through diversity. The Quran itself is a primary source of diversity. The Quranic term referring to **"different"** and **"difference"** occupies many verses. If belief is a coin, then, from the perspective of the new Islamic religious revolution, one side of that coin should read **"one-ness of God;"** the other **"diversity."**

For freedom of faith is the link between the two sides of that coin. No compulsion, no forced conversion, no use of force or the threat of such use to compel others to see faith through your own binoculars. The Quran instructs Muhammad to stay within the zone of being a messenger. Guidance is a godly prerogative. **"You (Muhammad) are not responsible for guiding them. But God guides whoever He pleases."**[188]

This thought structure (God's one-ness and diversity being the two sides of the same coin) banishes jihadism to global non-recognition. The same non-grata status accorded to jihadism also extends to Wahhabism as an incubator vehicle of jihadism. The underlying common denominator between the two unacceptable practices is forcing differences in belief into one mold where Islamic law is unrecognizable. Ignorance is the culprit.

This said, the complementarity between the three Abrahamic religions (Judaism, Christianity and Islam) confirms the role of knowledge. In this case the history of comparative religions becomes nearly a religious requirement. **"With Judaism's emphasis on the one-ness of God,**

---

[188] The Quran, Chapter 2, Verse 272.

Christianity's call for love, and Islam's advocacy of justice, one could see the close inter-relationship within a world based on shared values."[189]

Another important feeder into the interpretation of **"Read"** as meaning **"Learn"** is the role of Hekmah (Wisdom) as a source of Islamic Law. Wisdom is cultivated through knowledge. And the Quran itself puts almost at par with the Book, and with Muhammad's traditions. The Quran says: **"God is the One who has sent among the Unlettered a Messenger from among themselves, to recite His Revelations to them and to purify them, and to teach them the book and the Wisdom, though before they had been in manifest error."**[190]

The indelible linkage between the Quran and Hekmah is also emphasized by the late Islamic scholar, Gamal Al-Banna, where he says: **"Our judicial evidence on this point is that the Holy Quran links Wisdom (Hekmah) to itself as a source of law and faith. Any sound and thoughtful interpretation outside the Quranic verses should not be considered an aberration of what the Quran means. The Quran itself has resorted to Hekmah as a means of proper interpretation."**[191]

The effects of ignorance of the broad purposes of faith, any faith especially as regards to Islam, have proved to be devastating. Not only on the universal scale of jihadism (ISIS and the like); but also at the micro/local level. Honor killing is one example of this at the village level. Daily press reports bring also the news of mob action against those regarded as having offended Islam. One of the most astonishing examples of this **"micro jihadism,"** took place in Indonesia which is known for both diversity and tolerance within a 200 million Muslim community. At Bekasi, Indonesia, the mob is reported in late August 2017 to have beaten a man to death, then burned his body. Muhammad Al-Zahra (30 years of age) was suspected of having stolen an amplifier from a mosque. Refusing to accept his **"I'm not a thief,"** the hapless victim was killed to the triumphant cheers of the crowd. That is only one example of **"vigilante mobs continuing to**

---

[189] Gamal El-Banna, <u>Diversity Within An Islamic Community</u> (Cairo: Dar Al-Fikr Al-Islamic, 2001), p.24.

[190] <u>The Quran</u>, Chapter 62, Verse 2.

[191] El-Banna, <u>op. Cit.</u>, the Annex at page C, footnote #1.

torture and execute criminals."[192]

In his speech in Russia as the president of the **"Islamic Scholars Council"** (Hukama Al-Muslimoon), in August 2016, Dr. El-Taiyeb, the Grand Imam of Al-Azhar said: **"Issues of faith must be proven by logical evidence which do not permit of mere copying of earlier justifications. Such justifications are attributed to those who preceded us, but did not evolve beyond following literally the surface of texts."**[193]

That call for evolutionary thinking cannot prevail without continuing education. It helps Sharia be relevant to changing circumstances. This is the heart of ijtihad, the topic of the following presentation in this volume.

---

[192] <u>The New York Times</u>, August 31, 2017, p.A9.

[193] Dr. El-Taiyeb Speech in Chechnya, Russia, on August 25, 2017.

CHAPTER 15

Ijtihad: The Brain Power of Sharia

Islamic Law (Sharia) rests on a tripod. The Quran, Muhammad's tradition (Hadith), and Hekmah (Wisdom). Though the Quran in Islamic jurisprudence cannot be subject to controversy, the other two legs of that tripod do not have that total immunity. Nonetheless, Sharia, because of its need to evolve in order to be relevant to changing circumstances, has been reliant on Hekmah -ijtihad, in spite of it being, in certain types of ijtihad, non-consensual.

Such blemishes in ijtihad are overlooked in view of the Quran's assertion in many verses of the importance of Hekmah. As an example, the Quran says: **"Our Lord: send to them a Messenger from among them who shall recite Your Revelations to them, and teach them the Book (Quran) and the Wisdom and purify them; surely You are Almighty, All Wise."**[194] In fact there are references in the Quran to Hekmah, as a term and its derivatives, numbering nearly 120 times.

The centrality of Hekmah (the utilization of ijtihad) is made in the Quran as a vehicle for informing about Islam itself. **"Call mankind to the Way of your Lord with wisdom and sound advice, and reason with them in a well-mannered way."**[195] Arabic dictionaries define Al-Hekmah as **"Verbalism in consonance with correctness or the right path."**[196] Thus

---

[194] <u>The Quran</u>, Chapter 2, Verse 129.

[195] <u>Ibid.</u>, Chapter 16, Verse 125.

it connotes the analysis of the grounds and concepts expressing fundamental beliefs.

So ijtihad, which as an access to interpretation of the Islamic faith has never been closed, anchors its legitimacy in the primary source of Sharia, namely, the Quran. On this point, the Quran in its dialogue with the Virgin Mary regarding the birth of Christ: **"And He (God) will teach him (Jesus) the Book and the Wisdom and the Torah and the Bible (injeel)."**[197] Here the Quran expands the scope of ijtihad (interpretation by common sense) to cover all religions. Through that, it also treats all religions as equal, while affecting their continuum.

In his seminal book on **"The Life of Muhammad,"** Muhammad Hussein Haikal says: **"Islam has made of the human mind the arbiter in everything. It arbitrates in both religion and faith."**[198] The author here quotes from the Quran in affirmation the following: **"Those who disbelieve are like the one who cries out to one who only hears the sound of a call or a cry, deaf, dumb and blind, they do not understand."**[199]

Weighing in on the meaning of the aforementioned Quranic Verse, the great interpreter (Mujtahid) Sheikh Muhammad Abdoh (died in 1905) explains it as follows: **"That ayah (Verse or evidence) is clear on the fact that copying (meaning adhering to prior static explanations) without the use of either the mind or guidance through reason is indicative of disbelief."**

The main thought here is that no one can be a believer unless he/she understands faith through reason, thus securing self-awareness of it for the ultimate goal of conviction. Whoever has been raised on blind acceptance where the mind has no role, and on action without comprehension (fiqh) is not a believer... The aim of belief is to uplift the mind and the self through

---

[196] <u>Al-Monjid In Language and Information</u> (Beirut, Dar Al-Mashreq, 1997) 36 edition, p.146 (Arabic dictionary).

[197] <u>The Quran</u>, Chapter 3, Verse 48.

[198] Muhammad Hussein Haikal, <u>Life of Muhammad</u> (Cairo: Dar Al-Maarif, 2015), 25th edition, pp.412-413.

[199] <u>The Quran</u>, Chapter 2, Verse 171.

commensurate action. The person does the good act because he understands that such an act is pleasing to God (Allah). And he forsakes evil because he understands its negative consequences."[200]

Under the title of **"The Strength of Faith,"** Haikal calls this **"the enlightened faith."** By that term he means: **"Faith by someone who saw and reflected, then reflected again and again; until he reaches through that intuition the level of the enlightened faith."**[201] It i through ijtihad that a lethal weapon may until be fashioned to confront ISIS, Al-Qaeda, Al-Shabab, Boko Haram, and their franchises. Their murderous advocacy for violence as a means of glorifying Islam is nothing but a criminal hoax.

Even Islamic writers who have consistently shown support for the Muslim Brotherhood (a jihadi incubator), like Youssef Al-Qaradawi, with whom I share no common grounds, sees ijtihad from the same perspective as I see it. He states: **"There is no doubt that in order to make Sharia our legal arbiter, it is incumbent upon us to revive ijtihad. It is one basic tool for religious revival. Ijtihad is also a necessary mechanism to prove the breadth of Sharia concepts, its ability to cope with and guide its own evolution, and to help in solving problems faced by individuals and society in accordance with Islamic rules."**[202]

As a process of finding evidence, there are certain measurements for selecting the most probative one. The end result is unanimity (Ijmaa), meaning a broad agreement among qualified Islamic scholars of a specific region in regard to a certain issue. The Prophet Muhammad has said: **"My nation cannot be unanimous on what is wrong"** (by wrong meaning contradicting the Quran). However, the openness of Islam, where there is no Vatican or priestly intercessors, has made Ijmaa and analogy (qias), both of which are the main pillars of ijtihad, subjects of disagreement at times.

As noted above, there are measurements for selecting the best evidence. They may be encapsulated in **"to what extent does that interpretation serve the jurisdiction of the public good."** Here we are measuring the

---

[200] Haikal, op cit, p.412.

[201] Ibid., p.413.

[202] Youssef Al-Qaradawi, Contemporary Ijtihad, From Coherence To Scatteration (Cairo: Dar Al-Tawzee Wal Nashr Al-Islamiyah, 1994), p.3.

weight of evidence extrapolated by ijtihad, thus filling the gap left by Quranic verses or by Muhammad's tradition.

Al-Qaradawi summed these measurements in these words: **"The discovered rule should be in line with the times of its utterance; making it easy for people to apply; being as close as possible to the ease of practice manifest in Sharia; making it possible to effect the aims of Sharia, the public good, and the removal of corruption."**[203]

What makes jihadism extremely alien to the concepts of ijtihad, is that Islamic norms and practices are solidly based on ease not on making life difficult. **"God desires ease for you and not hardship."**[204] To this pronouncement should be added an authenticated Hadith by Muhammad: **"Make it easy not a hardship."**

In an open attack on jihadism, the Grand Imam of Al-Azhar, Dr. El-Taiyeb stated at a conference held in Cairo in 2016 for Burmese Muslim youth (Rohingya): **"God has created you, both the disbelievers and the believers ... Scholars of the Quran note that mentioning "the disbelievers" before "the believers" is indicative of the greater number of disbelievers as compared to the number of believers. We should learn that heavenly wisdom would not have intended that numbers superiority for disbelievers with a view of calling on the faithful to kill and eradicate them."**[205]

With regard to life events, where there was no text, these were disposed of by the Prophet himself. In preparation for the end of revelation and the Prophet's passing, Muhammad permitted his companions (Al-Sahabah) to resort to ijtihad. This is demonstrated by a famous dialogue between the Prophet and someone from Medina by the name of Moaz Ibn Jabal.

The Prophet had wished to assign Moaz to a judgeship in Yemen. Here is the translation of that job interview by the Prophet.

Question - **"If a case is brought to you, on what basis shall you judge?"**

---

[203] <u>Ibid</u>, p.20.

[204] <u>The Quran</u>, Chapte 2, Verse 185.

[205] El-Taiyeb speech for Burmese Muslim (Rohingya) in Cairo, December 2016.

Response - **"On the basis of the Quran - God's Book."**
Question - **"Suppose you did not find the answer for what you are looking** for?**"
Response - **"Then by the Sunna of God's Messenger."**
Question - **"But suppose you could not find the law determining the case, in either the Quran or the Sunna. How would you decide?"**
Response - **"Then by Ijtihad without delay."** (In Arabic: 'without delay' is **'La Aloo'** meaning also **'without hesitation')**

At the end of that interview, the comment by the Prophet was emblematic. Muhammad put his hands on his chest and uttered these words: **"Thanks be to God for having guided the Messenger of His Messenger to what is very satisfying for God and his Messenger."**[206]

We conclude from the above that: (1) Ijtihad in Islamic jurisprudence is a legitimate source for Sharia (The Quran, the Sunna, and ijtihad); (2) Because justice is a main pillar of Islam, the judge has to be conversant in the jurisdiction of matters on which there is no text; and (3) Ijtihad is like a flowing river whose waters keep Sharia forever green, forever evolving, and forever relevant. From all the above, the **Fatwa** in Islam has to be anchored in those sources.

Following up on the Prophet's instruction to Moaz upon appointing him as a judge in Yemen, the four Enlightened Caliphas (Al-Kholafa Al-Rashidoon) have followed the same bath. Abu-Bakr followed Omar's advice to get the Quran written; Omar's advice was simple. **"Collecting the Quran in one compendium was a good deed;"** Osman organized the words of God by Chapters and Ayahs in what became known as **"Musshaf Osman - the Book as gathered by Osman."** And Ali ensured that not one Ayah was missing. All the four acted on Ijtihad after the passing of the Prophet who left no tradition in that regard.

With that in mind, Omar in his famous legal instruction to his judge Shuraih demanded:
"Judge on the basis of the Quran. If you find no text on point, then judge by the Sunnah of God's Messenger (Rasool Illah). And if you find a non applicable text, then follow the precedents of good judges preceeding you. And if you still do not find what you are seeking, then strive to find the rule of law by your own thinking - your

---

[206] As quoted in multiple sources, including in Ibrahim Eissa, <u>A Blood Journey:The Early Assassins</u> (Cairo: Al-Karamah Lilnashr, 2016), p.25 (In Arabic).

ijtihad.[207]

Due to the fact that in ijtihad there is a continuous renewal of sharia for it to be applicable to continuously changing circumstances, there are basic requirements for someone to be a Mujtahid. First among these is the need for extensive scholarship in Islam and its sources, in the arts of Tafseer (interpretation), logic, Islamic history and its evolution, and the sociology of the environment. In Cairo for example, the Mufti (the premier Mujtahid) is second in rank to the Grand Imam of Al-Azhar. These requirements put charlatans like Bin Laden and his likes outside of that circle of specialized learning. Their fatwas are mere verbal frauds.

To acquire such diverse knowledge calls for discipline, continuity, perseverance, openness, recording, propagation, and assimilation of multiple sources. The mosque is **"Jamee"** - meaning an **"all inclusive"** place of worship; schooling; social interaction; growing your mind. For both men and women. This is the soul of ijtihad.

That flexibility in Islam, through ijtihad, is a sacred duty, **"Fareedha."** It is present not only in transactions, but also in worship. Muhammad said: **"Pray as you see me pray."** Then in connection with the Hajj ritual, the Prophet opened the door of variation wide. As he said: **"Do without fear."**

As has been noted above, Islamic Law has several characteristics. Among these is making of religious practices an easy endeavor. This is completely the opposite in what is called Wahhabi Islam. Since the primary role of ijtihad is continuously updating and reforming, hence describing it as **"the brain of Sharia,"** in neither Wahhabism, nor in jihadism is that brain in proper use. This is regardless of any type of ijtihad which manifests itself in various forms.

Now for some elaboration on the types of ijtihad. Ijtihad (Al-Hekmah) has two primary pillars: Ijmaa (unanimity) and Qiyas (analogy). In both of these, as well as in the Quran and the Sunnah, the main principle is **"Whatever is good for society."** Quranic reference to the jurisdiction of public good occurs in the following verse: **"Thus does God compare truth and falsehood; then as for the foam it vanishes, and that which is good for the people remains on the earth."**[208]

---

[207] Abbas Mahmoud Al-Akkad, <u>The Genius of Omar</u> (Cairo: Dar El-Helal, no date). In Arabic.

[208] <u>The Quran</u>, Chapter13, Verse 17.

This principle is dealt with extensively in a mountain of Islamic sources which deal with **"Fiqh Al-Masslaha"** - The jurisdiction of Societal Interest.

The jurisdiction of "Societal Interest" (Fiqh Al-Masslaha) has been lauded by highly notable Islamic scholars, like the late Gamal El-Banna. In his remarkable book, entitled, **"The Case For the New Fiqh,"** he regarded it as the basis for reaching correct judgement. Any conflict between this jurisdiction and the text would call for interpretation of the text through ijtihad.[209] It should be noted that this jurisdiction applies fully to Muslims and   non-Muslims   alike.

As to ijmaa, it is the consensus amongst qualified Muslim scholars in regard to the rule on an event occurring after the passing of the Prophet. In this regard,   the   Quran   says: **"O ye who believe! Obey God, and obey the Apostle, and those charged with authority among you."**[210] **"Those charged with authority"** are those scholars, fuqaha who are engaged in ijtihad.

Obviously, **"those charged with authority"** cannot, by any stretch of imagination, include the murderous gangs of terrorism. Starting with Bin Laden, and ending now with that insane Al-Baghdadi who claims to be the Caliphah of the so-called Islamic State (Daesh). They are not Muslim scholars, regardless of what they claim themselves to be. They are cut off the faith of Islam, because primarily Islam is based on inclusiveness, acceptance of all religions, tolerance, and engagement in whatever advances the interest of the world community. The jihadis do not abide by the Quranic high standard of **"faith is how you treat others."**[211] We see the reference to ijmaa in the Sunnah. The Prophet has said: **"My Umma (Nation) does not coalesce (meaning unite) on a consensus (ijmaa) based   on   evil."**[212]

---

[209] Gamal El-Banna, <u>The Case For a New Fiqh (Islamic Law)</u> (Cairo: Dar Al-Fikr Al-Islami, 2001), p.27. (In Arabic)

[210] <u>The Quran</u>, Chapter 4, Verse 59.

[211] A popular Islamic adage.

[212] An authentic Hadith by the Prophet Muhammad.

The other pillar of ijtihad is Qiyas (analogy). It means that issues on which no text can be found for guidance, could be settled in Sharia by analogy. Thus a Mujtahid tries to extrapolate from a text the intention of the judgment (the reasoning) in that text. As an example: The question of alcoholic beverages. In the Quran, it is stated: **"O ye who believe! Intoxicants and gambling, dedication of stones and divination by arrows are an abomination of Satan's handiwork: eschew (meaning avoid) such abomination that you may prosper."**[213]

By use of Al-Qiyas (analogy), Al-Mujtahid deduces the application of that rule to all matter, drinks or drugs, whether liquid or in pills or plants as **"Khamr" (intoxicant).** The reasoning here is that partaking of such substances affects the brain, and leads to irrationality. This is in addition to their deleterious effects on good judgement, and of taking care of oneself, one's family, one's community.

Aside from ijmaa and Qiyas, there are other types of ijtihad. These less prominent types of ijtihad end their list by including **"the legal methodology of other faiths which preceded Islam."**[214]

On that unity in faith, but diversity in practice, the Quran says: **"He has ordained for you the Religion which He commanded to Noah, and that We have revealed to you, and that which We commanded to Abraham, and Moses, and Jesus: Establish the Religion, and be not divided therein."**[215]

In summation, we should note that Islam is a faith and a community organizer within cooperative relationship with all others. Ijtihad is a basic pillar of Islamic law. The term **"umma"** means **"a community,"** not **"a State."**

Islam provides a balance between ritual/or worship, and secular transactions as may be governed by whatever is good for the community. That community is not the tribe. It is the human collectivity in which one resides. The Quran states: **"But seek, with the wealth which God has**

---

[213] The Quran, Chapter 5, Verse 90.

[214] Dr. El-Taiyeb,in his speech before the European Parliament on March 15, 2016, emphasized that continuity between all faiths.

[215] The Quran, Chapter 42, Verse 13.

bestowed on thee, the home of the hereafter, nor forget thy portion in this world. But do thou good, as God has been good to thee. And seek not occasion for mischief in the land. For God loves not those who do mischief."[216]

The most abhorrent type of mischief (fasad) is to take upon yourself the heinous task of declaring others as apostate. Or worse still, kill them in the name of Islam. 9/11 or the Paris massacres, or the Beirut butchery, or the death sentences issued by some so-called Islamic courts in Pakistan against **"blasphemers,"** are acts of aggression against Islam and the broader human   community.

The jurisdiction of public good is at the heart of the dynamism of Islam. And it is a primary source of its continuous renewal to make it accord with changing circumstances. Note that the Quran advises not only the Muslims, but humans in general. **"Al-Insan"** means **"the human being"** regardless of their faith is addressed in the Quran as **"O people."**

Al-Tawheed, the oneness of God, is the eternal tie between Islam and all other faiths, including Christianity and Judaism, and extending to non-revealed faiths such as the Sikh faith. **"Allahu Akbar" - "God is Great,"** is not a battle cry as ISIS or Al-Qaeda or Boko Haram claims. It means that we are all equal before God. He is the final judge. The final judge is not a so-called Calipha or a muallim, or a faqih, or anyone of these titles. Your link to your creator is a 24/7 hotline, direct, with no static; with a constant dial tone; without a broker between you and your Creator.

Furthermore, Ijtihad is essential as a basis for a pertinent Fatwa (an opinion based on Sharia). Islamophobia, have now degenerated into **"anti-Islamism"** is the byproduct of ignorance about Sharia. For its opponents, Sharia is perceived to be those crazy rules sputtering from the mouth of actors who know very little about Islam, a faith of universal values.

Finally it is incumbent upon all Muslims who reside outside of the lands of Islam to harmonize between their being Muslims and also being good citizens abiding by the legislated laws of their host States. That is the great lesson   of   the   Hijrah.   (immigration).

Those who call for the return of Islamic law and practice of more than 1400 years ago contribute to that anti-Islamism. No less than 38 American States

---

[216] The Quran, Chapter 28, Verse 77.

have unconstitutionally banned the mere mention of the word **"Sharia"** in their state courts. Their perspective is faulty. They look with apprehension at the brutal practices such as public beheading in certain Muslim countries. In those countries discrimination on the basis of gender, oppression of spouses and daughters and other females, floggings, cutting of human limbs, stoning for adultery, killing of secularists, and waging terrorism in the name of Islam, have caused a revulsion against Islam and deep suspicions of Muslims. These are all horrendous practices which are patently illegal under Islamic jurisprudence.

In Islamic law, Sharia, both the text and ijtihad are the daily open doors to whatever is reasonable, balanced, based on the good of society. That is the essence of Sharia - a constantly renewed system of laws with 80% commonality with the US Constitution. (see below). The Quran affirms: **"Those who disbelieve in Allah and His Messengers, and seek to make distinction between Allah and His Messengers, and say: We believe in some and disbelieve in others, and seek to close a way in between. Such are disbelievers in truth; and for disbelievers we prepare a shameful doom."**[217]

---

[217] <u>Ibid.</u>, Chapter 4, Verses 150 and 151.

CHAPTER 16

Jihad and Jihadism Are Not the Same

Jihad and jihadism are not the same. In fact the two terms are opposite to one another. Jihad is striving for betterment, and jihadism is a criminal endeavor intended to foil others from reaching their lawful goals. Because of the lack of understanding of the fine points of this terminology, not only by non-Muslims, but also by Muslims, jihadism preempted the field of interfaith unity and understanding.

Having begun in earnest following the expulsion of Soviet forces from Afghanistan in 1989, jihadism became the criminal protocol of Bin Laden's Al-Qaeda which spawned several others in its wake. The initial main salvo was the destruction of the American embassies in Kenya and Tanzania in 1998. But the lines of persistent confrontation by both arms and other forceful means were drawn as a consequence of the criminal attacks on the US on September 11, 2001 (9/11). That was the start of both globalizing the war on jihadism and the entrenchment of anti-Islamism.

Unfortunately the fear of jihadi assaults, which became nearly free-lance affairs following the organizational disintegration of Al-Qaeda, ISIS, Al-Shabab and the like, has focused world attention on **"jihad,"** not on ijtihad. There is of course a clear connotation of human striving in these two terms. But ijtihad, as could be seen in the preceding chapter, is striving for moving Sharia forward with the times; while **"jihad"** as jihadism is criminal striving for reflecting Islam as a faith for the sword, of the sword, and by the sword.

Thus the Grand Imam of Al-Azhar, Dr. El-Taiyeb, in launching the new Islamic religious revolution, which was energized by Egypt's Presidential El-Sisi as a cardinal principle of the reconstruction of the New Egypt, has repeatedly invoked the huge danger of jihadism to world peace. In his speech before the European Parliament in Berlin, Dr. El-Taiyeb said: **"Whoever understands the teaching of the Prophet Muhammad outside the framework of mercy for all and of universal peace, is ignorant of Islam, its ethos, and is doing harm to that faith."**[218]

From there, the Grand Imam of Al-Azhar pivoted to the definition provided by Islamic Law (Sharia) of jihad. So he said: **"In Islam, Jihad is not limited to battling for repelling aggression. This is the lower jihad. The higher jihad is the striving for self-rectification and for freedom from bad impulses."** El-Taiyeb ideological coup de grace to jihadism was delivered in what followed in his speech in Berlin. He said: **"The concept of legitimate jihad in Islamic law includes every effort exerted for the public good. The first among such efforts is the struggle to do away with poverty, ignorance, diseases, namely whatever is done to help the poor and the destitute."**

His linking the Islamic concept of legitimate jihad to the jurisdiction of the public good was akin to separating between **"sky above"** and **"mud below,"** the latter is an apt description of the criminal acts of jihadis all over the world. Again, we find in the use by jihadis of the term **"jihad"** another example of terrorist organizations highjacking a noble term for sordid ends. Here again the danger is compounded by the adoption by non-Muslims of the jihadi vocabulary and applying it to the entire body of Islam.

Again to quote from that speech in Berlin: **"What is being said about jihad in Islam as an activity whereby arms are raised to fight non-Muslims, to stalk them, and to liquidate them, is but an abomination. It is very regrettable that such utterly mistaken understanding and interpretation of the Quran's provisions and of the Prophet's tradition is spread far and wide in order to hurt the faith of Islam and Muslims."**

In the jihadi ideology, we find veneration of the deep past as a guide to the future.[219] This is salafi thinking, meaning that the best of Islam, in fact the best believers in Islam, were the ancestors (the salaf). Here we find an ideological link between salafism, Wahhabism, and jihadism. Such link is

---

[218] El-Taiyeb's speech in Berlin, March 15, 2016.

[219] Gamal El-Banna, <u>The Strategy of Islamic Advocacy In the 21st Century</u> (Cairo: Dar Al-Fikr Al-Islami, 2000), pp.50-53 (In Arabic)

fortified by interpreting the Quran and the Hadith (Muhammad's tradition) in the context of the tribalism which has seeped into some Islamic beliefs and practices. This is evident in Salafi thinking about other religions, and about women, the role of the Ruler, and the concept of veneration through ijtihad.

Such thought has been delegitimated by the Quran as idolatory. One Quranic verse says: **"And when it is said to them, 'Come to what God has revealed, and to the Messenger,' They said, 'Sufficient for us is the way we found our fathers doing.' Even though their fathers knew nothing and were not guided."**[220] Again the Quran abhors a return to an unenlightened past as it says: **"But they say: 'We found our fathers following a way, and we are only guided by their footsteps.'"**[221]

Anti-jihadism thus drives towards a continually evolving interpretation of Islam which accords with the constant changes of the realities of a world of constant change. A former head of Egypt's Ministry of Entails (Awqaf)(Religious Affairs), Dr. Mahmoud Zakzouk writes as follows: **"The alternative to renewal is stagnancy. This means inactivity of life, which is impossible because life and motion are like inseparable full brothers... Thus renewal in Islamic jurisprudence is always needed. In addition to this, new cases arise which former Islamic jurists did not hear and which, therefore, require new reasoning and a deep search in order to issue suitable legal judgments for them."**[222]

The ideological clash between the thought reflected by Al-Azhar and affiliates like Zakzouk's Supreme Council for Islamic Affairs, on the one hand, and jihadism thought on the other, is manifest in western writings about that clash. In those writings, more weight is given to the latter than the former. Anti-jihadism, which is mostly expressed in Arabic, does not get its due recognition in western literature. Nor is the literature coming out from the Al-Azhar and similar institutions readily available in the west as it is expressed in either Arabic or in non-absorbable English.

---

[220] The Quran, Chapter 5, Verse 104.

[221] Ibid., Chapter 43, Verse 22.

[222] Mahmoud Zazouk, Objectives of Islamic Shariah and the Need for Renewal (Cairo: Ministry of Al-Awqaf/The Supreme Council for Islamic Affairs, 2007), pp. 26-27.

An example of western literature which tips the scales in favor of reflecting jihadi thought as the prevalent mode of Islamic thought is David Horowitz's book entitled **"Unholy Alliance: Radical Islam and the American Left."** Relying on statements by a Palestinian professor and Muslim Brother by the name of Abdullah Azzam, in his magazine called Al Jihad, Horowitz quotes Azzam as saying: **"This duty (duty of jihad) shall not lapse with victory in Afghanistan, and the jihad will remain an obligation until all other lands which formerly were Muslim come back to us and Islam reigns within them once again."**[223]

Horowitz's book was advertised as a **"New York Times Bestseller."** Compare that privileged status to the under-privileged status of Al-Azhar document called **"The Documents of Al-Azhar Al-Shareef;"** the anti-terrorism conventions issued in 1998 and 1999 by both the League of Arab States (LAS) and the Organization of the Islamic Conference (OIC) respectively, or publications such as **"Islam Between Truth and False Allegations"** by a consortium of Muslim Scholars. Though in English, such Islamic authentic publications do not find their way into the huge and complex publications distribution and marketing in the west.

These are the inaudible voices of reason about ani-jihadism. Samples of these historic voices follow: **"Recognition of Al-Azhar Al-Shareef as the authoritative focal point to which issues of Islam, its sciences, its legacies, and its juridical ijtihad and thought are referred."**[224] Rebutting the allegation that Muslims are urged **"to inflict harm upon others,"** a consortium of Islamic scholars assert that: **"Both the Quranic texts and the Prophet's sayings call for a peaceful co-existence with non-Muslims."**[225]

Note should also be taken of Dr. El-Taiyeb speech in Paris in June 3, 2016, at the Second Dialogue Between the Scholars of East and West. In that speech, Al-Azhar's Grand Imam referred to the terrorist act in Paris in December 2015 in these words: **"A few months ago, beautiful and**

---

[223] David Horowitz, <u>Unholy Alliance: Radical Islam and the American Left</u> (Washington, D.C.: Regnery Publishing, Inc. 2006), pp.140-141.

[224] Al-Azhar's Document on the Future of Egypt, Principle #11, Cairo, August, 8, 2011.

[225] <u>Ahmed Shalabi, et al</u>, "Islam Between Truth and False Allegations," (Rabat: The Islamic Educational, Scientific and Cultural Organization, 1997), p.74.

luminous Paris suffered a dark night when it lost about 140 lives. There blood was shed in an instant, together with 168 others as a result of terrorism. None, whether in the east or the west, would disagree regarding the denunciation of the perpetrators who derided human innate decency and all the teachings of religious, custom and laws."[226]

There is no doubt in that the case of fighting Soviet occupation of Afghanistan in the 1970's and 1980's was a permissible right to self-defense. Under Islamic law, as in all types of international law, self-defense in cases of foreign aggression or internal dictatorial oppression is authorized. But following the expulsion of the USSR from Afghanistan, the **"mujahideen"** of that period became the terrorists of Al-Qaeda. Under Bin Laden and Al-Zawahiri, global terror became an industry using Islam as a shield. Herein lies the ideological break between defensive jihad and criminal terrorism.

How many news outlets or even scholars and experts in terrorism have heard of **"The Arab Convention on the Suppression of Terrorism,"** signed in Cairo on April 1998? This is an example of the proverbial **"dialogue of the deaf,"** between the Muslim and non-Muslim worlds. A denial of the fact that where jihadism was instigated is also where, through the proper means of resistance, it is being confronted. Though terrorism/jihadism has no unified consensual definition, the Arab inter-State community has reached in that convention an acceptable elaboration of the meaning of that term.

Part One of that Convention, defines the term terrorism (an interchangeable term with jihadism) as follows: **"Any act or threat of violence, whatever its motives or purposes, that occurs for the advancement of an individual or collective criminal agenda, causing terror among people, causing fear by harming them, or placing their lives, liberty or security in danger, or aiming to cause damage to the environment or to public or private installations or property or to occupy or seize them, or aiming to jeopardize a national resource."**[227]

---

[226] El-Taiyeb's speech, the Second Dialogue Between World Scholars, Paris, France, June 3, 2016. (In Arabic).

[227] "The Arab Convention on the Suppression of Terrorism," signed in Cairo on April 22, 1998, and deposited with the General Secretariat of the League of Arab States. (Cairo, Egypt) Part I, Article 2.

This is the very spirit of the language of the New Islamic Religious Revolution. As expounded by the Grand Imam, Dr. El-Taiyeb, who said in Nigeria where Boko Haram has committed all types of atrocities: **"There is no guidance in the sick and purposefully confusing perceptions which depict Islam as a faith hungry for blood-letting, violation of women, taking females hostage, kidnapping young girls and trafficking for sales in markets. These are scenes which are most shameful and for which virtue, custom and religion should weep."**[228] Apt words directed against horrific events perpetrated by Boko Haram, which means **"non-Islamic learning is sinful."**

Here follows the Quranic verse which is often cited by Muslim UN delegates during debates on these central issue: **"Because of that we prescribed to the Children of Israel that whoever kills a soul, unless it be for retaliation or because of spreading corruption on earth, it would be as if he had killed all mankind, and whoever saves a life, it would be as if he had saved the life of all mankind."**[229]

Jihadi victims all over the world have not been confined to humans -mostly uninvolved civilians. The jihadis, whether organizations or individual freelancers, have also targeted museums, monuments, places of worship, market places, schools, hospitals, aid givers, first responders, vacationers, and even Muslim immigrants fleeing for their lives into Europe and the Americas. A worldwide senseless campaign of nihilism under the cover of Islam. Describing Islam as a faith by Dr. El-Taiyeb called it **"a faith of peace. Not only peace for humankind. But peace extended also to animals, plants, and inanimate objects."**[230]

If we were to sum up jihadism in the context of a global insurrection, we need to frame it in concise questions and answers: (i) What is an insurrection.? It is the total collapse of law and order; conflict without rules; targets without choice; terror intended to generate mass fear; (ii) Is it seeking governance? No!! It is seeking raw power which is in constant shift. If it attempts to govern, as was the case during its heyday of ISIS in Raqqa and Mosul, it uses the civilians of those areas as human shields for its own protection.

---

[228] Dr. El-Taiyeb, Speech in Abuja, Nigeria, May 2016.

[229] The Quran, Chapter 5, Verse 32.

[230] El-Taiyeb, op. cit., Abuja, Nigeria. May 2016.

Continuing with this summary as questions and answers: (iii) What are their bylaws? Jihadis claim that Islam is **"uber alles"** (above all) other religions. Their Islam is sectoral -selective jihadi Islam. No shiism, no secularism; no ijtihad; the sword is the arbiter of differences; Islam is a facilitator for terrorism; and women are inferior beings who have to be kept behind walls or covered by black from head to toe, except for slits for the eyes to see.

Without further enumeration, jihadism has used for its terrorism ideology all types of social media; traded in stolen oil resources and drugs; lured to its ranks the uninitiated young, especially females for the comfort of their soldiers; and used the chaos engulfing the Arab Middle East to move into areas where central authority had either vanished or was vanquished. Rape is a jihadi weapon of war; and the use of European and American recruits with roots in the Middle East is a valuable instrument -a new type of a **"fifth column."**[231]

There is nothing in the Quran or the Hadith that could support jihadism. On the contrary, the entire concept of the use of force in matters of faith is totally un-Islamic. The Quran addresses Muhammad rhetorically to shun completely any use of coercion to gain adherents. It says: **"And if your Lord had pleased, whoever is on the earth would have believed, all of them together. Would you then compel the people to become believers?"**[232]

The essence of the above is that there can be no charges of apostasy. This is because it is a judgement which cannot be levelled by any human being against another. Islam leaves such judgement entirely in the hands of the Creator. Any human arrogating such power to themselves is, from the prism of the new Islamic religious revolution, an outlaw. On that basis there is no measurement of faith in the Quran except piety -piety in all stripes and variations, without having to be only Islamic. Again to the Quran: **"O mankind! We have created you from a male and a female, and made you nations and tribes, that you may know one another. Surely the most honorable of you in the sight of God is the most pious of you.**

---

[231] Based on my presentation at an international panel held in Toronto on May 7, 2017 under the aegis of our non-profit SUNSGLOW - Global Training In the Rule of Law.

[232] The Quran, Chapter 10, Verse 99.

Indeed God is All-Knowing, All-Aware."[233]

No wonder that the above quotation from the Quran is beautifully framed in a wood carving, donated by the Government of Morocco to the UN where it is exhibited at the approaches to the General Assembly hall. A clear call to interfaith and inter-ethnic amity on a global scale which defeats the jihadi call for combat in the name of an Islam which the Quran and Muhammad's Tradition do not condone.

It is for all these reasons that jihad and jihadism are not the same. The former has well defined parameters: self-policing and self-defense. The latter is an insurrection which hides its criminal terrorism behind Islam. Here we should cite a contemporary example on why, in the context of jihad, oppression could generate an activity on the part of the oppressed which might be misunderstood as terrorism. This is an example of the Myanmar military persecution of the Muslim Rohingyas, forcing them out of their homes and villages, and causing nearly half a million of them to flee for their lives to neighboring Bangladesh.

Being a religious minority within a Buddhist majority, it has been disheartening to see the mass exodus by the Rohingyas into an adjoining Muslim country, in what the UN and human rights organizations have characterized as ethnic cleansing. In that special context, we find the Quranic exception for the use of force as legitimate jihad for self-defense.

The Quran sanctions jihad (not jihadism) as a tool of self-defense against lawless authoritarian persecution of Muslims, in this case the Rohingyas. It calls upon the oppressed to resist. The injunction against raising the sword is removed by the Quran in self-defense cases. It says: **"only with regard to those who have fought you in the cause of Religion, and expelled you from your homes, and have helped in expelling you, that you should take them for friends. And whoever takes them for friends, those are the evildoers."[234]**

This 4-year old military confrontation, though between the weak (Rohingyas), and one of Asia's biggest armies (the Burmese army), shall undoubtedly open the door for the jihadis outside Myanmar to radicalize the Rohingyas. Unfortunately the government of Myanmar (Burma) is

---

[233] <u>Ibid</u>, Chapter 49, Verse 13.

[234] <u>Ibid</u>, Chapter 60, Verse 9.

unwittingly aiding in the conversion of an incipient jihad into jihadism. Said an university-educated Rohingya now living in Bangladesh: **"Why does Burma call us terrorists? It's one word: Islam"**[235]

What adds to the global effects of this vicious cycle, leading from self-defense to radicalization, is the blame heaped upon the victim by the President of Myanmar, Ms. Aung San Suu Kyi. She, a Nobel Peace Prize laureate, claimed without proof, that the Rohingyas and their supporters have created **"an iceberg of misinformation."**[236] But the flow of Rohingya refugees into impoverished Bangladesh points the finger of blame to the Burmese military.

As the universal ramifications of jihadism, even when it begins as jihad, become clearer, the voice of the new Islamic religious revolution gets also to be more audible. Its strength comes from this injunction against aggression which gives rise to all kinds of negative reactions against Islam and Muslims everywhere. The Quran admonishes: **"And fight in God's cause those who fight you, and do not transgress. Surely God does not love the transgressors."**[237] Thus, even in legitimate resistance to authoritarianism or foreign occupation seeking to uproot whole communities of citizens from their ancestral lands, the Islamic call for proportionality is made.

At its annual session held in Cairo in January, 2016, the Egyptian Council for Foreign Affairs made the following conclusion: **"The attempt to Islamize terrorism (jihadism) is in vain. Terrorism is not caused by Islam. Yet the terrorist uses Islam as a cushion, a pretext for his terroristic behavior. Hence the strategy to confront terrorism should focus on identifying the environment which incentivizes terrorism and creates a climate for jihadism."**[238]

---

[235] As quoted in the <u>New York Times</u>, Sept.18, 2017, p.A.1 and p.A11.

[236] <u>Ibid</u>, p.A.11.

[237] <u>The Quran</u>, Chapter 2, Verse 190.

[238] The Egyptian Council for Foreign Affairs (ECFA), <u>Egypt and the Challenges of Terrorism</u> (Cairo: January 18, 2016, Thirteenth Annual Session), p.130. In Arabic.

CHAPTER 17

Equal Justice For All Before the Law

The gulf of misunderstanding between Muslims and non-Muslims stems from ignorance by both parties of what justice in Islam is all about. The Muslims regard the Quran and the Hadith as the primary sources of law (Sharia). Primary does not mean exclusive, since interpretation (ijtihad) is another source of Sharia. Nonetheless, the non-Muslims swallow without vetting the misinterpretation by the jihadists of what justice in Islam is based on.

The result: The term **"Sharia Law"** (a semantic redundancy) has become in non-Muslim societies a weapon of fear. Leaving the manifestations of this fear for the following chapter, one finds the term justice (ADL) occurs in the Quran 28 times. The Prophet Muhammad was the first judge. Addressed to the Prophet, the Quranic instruction for him was: **"And say: 'I believe in whatever Book God has revealed. I have been commanded to do justice between you. God is our Lord and your Lord.'"**[239] In that verse alone, one finds a clear indication of Quranic affirmation of all faiths, together with leaving the matter of 'judicial review' regarding issues of faith to God.

Another Quranic verse makes justice a manifestation of piety. **'O you who believe! Be constant for God as just witnesses, and do not let detestation of a people move you to be unfair; be equitable; that is close to piety, and for God, God is well aware of all that you do.'**[240]

---

[239] <u>The Quran</u>, Chapter 42, Verse 15.

[240] <u>Ibid</u>, Chapter 5, Verse 8.

Thus **"witnessing"** (the rendering of whatever has been discerned or heard truthfully) becomes probative if underpinned by objective, not emotional criteria.

These heavenly commands, which ensure equal justice for all before the law, are today memorialized above the bench seating judges throughout the Arab/Muslim world. Being the equivalent in American courts of **"In God We Trust,"** these plaques declare: **"When you judge between people, that you judge with justice."**[241]

Furthermore, every Imam (prayer leader) ends his sermon as he descends from the pulpit to lead his congregation in prayer, repeats this verse as a pre-prayer opener: **"Most surely God enjoins justice, the doing of good deeds and generosity to near of kin, and He forbids indecency, abomination and tyranny. He admonishes you that you may remember."**[242]

It was therefore an affirmation of these principles of justice, that the Second Caliph, Omar Ibn Al-Khattab, issued his famous instructions to the judiciary (See Annex I). It was in connection with his appointment of Abu-Musa Al-Ashaari, judge for Kofa, Iraq. Summing up its main principles, in this author's translation from the original Arabic, Omar instructions, paraphrased as follows: (1) Understand the pleadings, and enforce your judgement when certain of its correctness; (2) There is no benefit to the community to speak of rights which are not enforced; (3) Ensure a look of neutrality in your facial expression. This shall discourage a well-known person from expecting your injustice, or a destitute from anticipating your unfairness.

Then Omar moves on to the heart of his judicial decree as he postulates: (4) The burden of evidence is on the plaintiff, while a denial by a defendant must be backed up by a solemn oath; (5) conciliation (without litigation) is permissible unless it is a settlement **which approves** whose principles contrary to scripture, or nullifies a sanction which is permitted; (6) Do not hesitate to change a judgment you issued the day before, but upon review, you discover it to be defective. For right is intrinsic and cannot be abrogated by the passage of time. Other provisions follow in that historic

---

[241] Ibid, Chapter 4, Verse 58.

[242] Ibid, Chapter 16, Verse 90.

document which adorns in Arabic the entrance to many courtrooms.[243]

In his book, **Islam: Faith and Law**, a former Grand Imam of Al-Azhar, Mahmoud Shaltout, ends his seminal book by addressing the judiciary in the context of Islam as being underpinned by evidence. In this regard, that great Islamic scholar states that: **"A ruler who is not steeped in the ways to evidence and their circumstances causes the loss of many rights and delivers judgements which the populace knows to be invalid."** He even cites the story of Joseph who was sold by his brothers as a slave to an Egyptian pharaoh. Here he cites **"Joseph shirt"** as an evidence exculpating Joseph from the false charge of sexual assault raised by the pharaoh's wife.[244]

Even the most conservative of Sharia experts cannot deny that there is room for interpretation of the Quran and the Hadith. One of these is Dr. Youssef Qasim of Cairo University who expounds the following: **"The Almighty God has decreed for his subjects the total and permanent rules which are not subject to change or alteration. But He left the details for Sharia scholars and other public officials to extrapolate comprehensive rules in accordance with conditions of their societies."[245]**

One of the main principles of adjudication in Muslim societies urges the judge to be defendant oriented. This principle is anchored in the general rule of **"whatever is not specifically forbidden is allowed."** Applying this rule to culinary matters, we find that Sharia is more lenient than its application by Muslim practices.

This is evidenced by the Quranic advisory to Muhammad. **"They ask you what is permitted for them, say, 'Permitted to you is all that is good and pure... All that is good and pure has today been permitted to you, and the food of the people of earlier scriptures is permissible to**

---

[243] Omar's Instructions to the Judiciary, addressed upon his appointing of a judge for Kofa, Iraq.

[244] The Grand Imam Mahmoud Shaltout, <u>Islam: Faith and Law</u> (Cairo, Dar Al-Shrouk, 2015)21st edition, pp.464-465.

[245] Youssef Qasim, <u>Principles of Islamic Jurisprudence</u> (Cairo: Dar Al-Nahdha Al-Arabiyyah, 1997); p.57

you, and your food is permissible to them."[246]

We note here also the persistence of the Quran in its description of Islam as a continuation of all prior religions. Because of the centrality of that precept of inter-faith parity and amity, the following Quranic verse bears repetition. **"And We revealed to you the Book (The Quran) in Truth, confirming what has remained intact of the Scripture before it, and the determiner of it. So judge between them according to what God has revealed, and do not follow their vain desires, turning aside from the Truth that has come to you."**[247]

It could therefore be seen that the judiciary in Islamic jurisprudence is guided by the Quran, Muhammad's traditions, and the vast area of ijtihad which is based on interpretation of both rules and custom. Regarding the latter, there are two mutually reinforcing legal concepts which are universally applicable. These are **"No Crime Without Law"** (in latin: Ni Crimen Sin Leges), and **"Laws Are Subservient to Custom"** (in latin: Leges Mori Serviunt). The exception to this standard is that custom should not contravene scripture. Contrary to jihadi lunacy, there is a need for laws, for prevailing custom, for evidence, for acceptance of the other. There is also a need for recognition that faith is non-negotiable, that all beliefs stand on the same footing of equality, thus commanding mutual and universal respect. For jihadis to practice in the name of Islam extrajudicial killing, destruction of places of worship and other communal monuments, and butchery while screaming **"Allahu Akbar"** there is nothing left but the evisceration of all human qualities.

The test of the jihadi rebellion against all of humanity could also be seen in their total rejection of evidence on their horrendous claims. In Islamic law (Sharia), evidence is central. It consists of all the means by which any alleged matter of fact, the truth of which is submitted to investigation through judicial trial, is established or disproved. As has been noted above, the word **"Ayah"** in the Quran means **"evidence."** In jihadism, which has tried but failed in hijacking Islam, there is no such thing.

One of the main features in adjudication in Muslim societies, which parallels that in non-Muslim communities, is the exception of dire necessity. It applies to both rituals and transactions. The Quran provides as follows:

---

[246] <u>The Quran</u>, Chapter 5, Verses 4 and 5.

[247] <u>Ibid.</u>, Chapter 5, Verse 48

"But whoever is constrained by necessity, not out of insolence, nor with the intention of repeating it, then no sin is on him. Surely God is All-Forgiving, All-Merciful."[248] The necessity exception is at one end of the act; forgiveness and mercy are at the other end. Such symbiotic relationship between cause or case and its effect is a hallmark of justice, not only in Islam but also in other traditions. This is a central feature of co-existence which helped to catapult Islam out of parched Arabia to much broader civilizations beyond it.

If we were to compare the concept of equal justice for all before the law as it exists in Islamic societies to the same concept as perceived by non-Muslim societies, we find the difference between the two concepts not in the substance, but in the source of those concepts. This is to say that substantially the two concepts are one and the same. The only difference is that in Muslim societies one finds the concept largely rooted in the relationship between God and the human. But in non-Muslim societies, the concept flows from the people.[249]

The oft-repeated invocation of God in **"Allahu Akbar,"** especially in non-jihadi setting, could be regarded as the equivalent of **"Power To the People."** In a dialogue with His Holiness the late Pope Shenouda of the Coptic Church, he asked me this question: **"Where does the law come from?".** In the presence of a large audience, my response was a compromise between the two concepts. After saying: **"Law comes from God,"** his follow-up question was **"Then what happened to it?" "Then it became natural law, then customary law, then transcribed (written) law,"** was my response. Smilingly, His Holiness said: **"You should come have a cup of coffee with me in Cairo at the St. Mark Cathedral."**

Needless to add here is that from whatever source justice in general, or law in particular, have come from, the critical element is the application of law in a manner that could be seen as fulfilling justice. A vital area of transactions which calls for predicted enforcement is the area of contract law.[250] The importance of contract law is specifically evidenced by several

---

[248] <u>Ibid</u>., Chapter 2, Verse 173.

[249] Sofi Abutaleb, **"Shura and Democracy,"** A presentation at the School of Law, University of Mansourah, Egypt, April 1999, p.70.

[250] See Muhammad Naguib Al-Moghrabi, <u>The Theory of Contracts in Islamic Jurisprudence</u> (Cairo: Dar Al-Nahdah Al-Arabiyyah, 2003).

Quranic verses. One such verse is in Chapter 5 of the Quran where it says: **'O you who believe! Fulfill thy pledges'**[251](meaning contracts).

Another verse, which regards treaties as contracts, states: **"Those with whom you have made treaties, and who violate them every time, they have not the fear of God."**[252] The Quran also points to contracts as a generalized commitment, in fact a mode of behavior. In that sense, it provides: **"And do not approach the property of the orphan, except in the most fair way, until he reaches maturity. And fulfill your commitments; surely you shall be questioned about the commitments."**[253]

It is in the context of joining justice, law and morals that the Prophet Muhammad gained, well before he began his advocacy of Islam, the approbation of being called **"honest."** Such commendation which was bestowed upon him by Quraish, his tribe, was earned by Muhammad as a bailee with whom traders and others (bailors) entrusted with their properties. Such characterization could not be but an asset to the credibility of Muhammad, in Arabia of 1400 years ago. Even before the unfortunate rise of jihadism, equality before the law has suffered its utmost retreat in regard to minority rights and the empowerment of women. Human history has proven that violation of minority rights has led to instability and state fragmentation. This is evidenced by the most recent case of South Sudan splitting from the Sudan, due to the Islamist rule in Khartoum. We also have the unfortunate cases of possible territorial fragmentation in Syria, Libya, and Yemen. And the denial of gender equality has led to the retardation of national development, as in the case of the domineering role of Wahhabism in Saudi Arabia.

Against these development retardants, (denial of minority rights, and of gender equality), the new Islamic religious revolution has sounded the alarm. It was in the voice of the Grand Imam of Al-Azhar, Dr. El-Taiyeb, who addressed the calamity of denial of human rights of the Rohingyas in a Cairo conference held for their youth. He said: **"This crisis is truly strange, especially for the people of Myanmar (Burma). For that is a people who have deep roots since eternity in the history of religion,**

---

[251] The Quran, Chapter 5, Verse 1.

[252] Ibid., Chapter 8, Verse 56.

[253] Ibid., Chapter 17, Verse 34.

wisdom and peace. They have previously taught humanity a great deal. Their civilization and religions were torches for peace for humanity everywhere."[254] What lent more weight to that statement is that it was made before the general conference of Islamic Scholars (Hukama - wisemen) which took place in Cairo.

In regard to women empowerment, Dr. El-Taiyeb attacked gender inequality at a world summit held in the United Arab Emirates in 2016. The event was a conclave of 50 women heading their parliaments in various parts of the world. The head of that 11th Summit for parliamentary speakers who convened that summit was Dr. Amal Al-Qubaisi, speaker of the UAE Parliament. In his statement, Dr. El-Taiyeb looked forward to the empowerment of women through that summit as a weapon against jihadism. The timing of that statement nearly coincided with the perpetration of a terrorist act against the Copts while at prayer in their church in Egypt.

Quoting from that statement by the Grand Imam of Al-Azhar would reflect the linkage made through the new Islamic religious revolution between equality before the law, women empowerment and the struggle against jihadism.

Dr. El-Taiyeb said: **"Arcane custom and tradition have been, in some instances, unaffected by the clear provisions of the Quran which exalt the status of women, scientifically, socially and in humanitarian endeavors... Those so-called schools of thought (mazhab) have nearly returned women to their pre-Islamic status. It thus nullified many of their rights guaranteed for them by Islam. It engineered a strange legality for a siege which caused women to nearly getting accustomed to their solitude and isolation."**[255]

It is of particular interest that Dr. El-Taiyeb, in his UAE speech, quoted the Prophet Muhammad as saying, perhaps rhetorically: **"If I were to be compelled to make a preference in the matter of gender, I would prefer women to men."** The Grand Imam of Al-Azhar followed up by a clarification of that Hadith by saying: **"The Hadith was intended to draw**

---

[254] Dr. El-Taiyeb, Speech on Dialogue for Peace, Cairo Conference For Burmese Youth, December/January 2017. (In Arabic)

[255] _____, speech at the World Summit of Women Speakers of Parliament, the United Arab Emirates; 2016.

attention to particular qualities and talents where women outdo men."[256]

In the same vein, the late Islamic scholar, Gamal El-Banna, authored an entire book entitled: **"The Muslim Woman: Between Her Liberation By the Quran, And Her Restriction By the Fuqaha (Islamic Scholars)."**[257] The author had dedicated that book to his sister Fawziah El-Banna who had predeceased him, in 1997. The thrust of the thesis of that book is that the status of women in law and society is fully co-equal to men. Citing many Quranic verses in support of **"justice for all,"** the author included the following: **"And the believing men and the believing women, they are the friends of each other, they enjoin good and forbid evil."**[258]

Modern constitutions in the Muslim world have upheld the universality of **"equal justice for all before the law."** A prime example of these constitutions is that of Egypt, following its liberation in July 2013 from the yoke of Islamist rule by the Muslim Brotherhood.

The preamble of that Constitution promulgated on January 18, 2014, states: **"We are inscribing a Constitution which, while asserting that the principles of sharia are the main source of legislation, the point of reference to their interpretation is what is guaranteed by the decisions of the Supreme Constitutional Court. It is a Constitution which ensures the opening before us of the path to the future, and accords with the Universal Declaration of Human Rights in the drafting of which we took part and to which we acceded ... A Constitution which affects equality for all in rights and obligations without discrimination."**[259]

In none of the arguments and evidence produced above could one find any

---

[256] <u>Id</u>.

[257] Gamal El-Banna, <u>The Muslim Woman: Between Her Liberation By the Quran, And Her Restriction By the Islamic Scholars</u> (Cairo: Dar Al-Fikr Al-Islami, No Date)

[258] <u>The Quran</u>, Chapter 9, Verse 71.

[259] The 2014 Constitution of the Arab Republic of Egypt, January 18, 2014; Preamble.

commonality with the murderous ideology of jihadism, against which the new Islamic religious revolution has been launched in earnest as of 2014.

CHAPTER 18

Anti-Islamism Fuels Jihadism

From Trump's Muslim bans to other advocates of anti-Islamism, jihadism world-wide gets plenty of oxygen. Hatred begets hatred, as the cycle of global violence spins out of control. That oxygen flows through many pipelines. These include the rise of the right of all stripes in America, Europe and even Asia (e.g. Myanmar). Compounding the problem are anti-immigration, anti-refugees fleeing a dysfunctional Middle East and West Africa, and the rise of American and European neo-Nazism, especially in the form of anti-semitism. Even channels funded by Russia for influencing the 2016 American presidential elections in favor of Trump constitute part of the universal rise of the anti-Islamism dangerous tide. The new name of Islamophobia is anti-Islamism.

Focusing on America, we find plenty of examples. In these examples, whether presidential bans on Muslims, or incendiary statements by people in authority, or mere silence in the face of provoking Muslims, the ugly patterns are worrisome. The more the Muslim world hangs tough in confronting jihadism, the more stupid those anti-Islamists become in stoking the fires of hatred. It is like the people whose house is on fire by jihadi arsonists are directing their blazing guns at the Muslim fire brigades and trucks rushing to save them.

Let us view the tragic panorama of anti-Islamism fueling jihadism. Here we are confronted by a form of cultural genocide -the ideology of obliterating the values of **"the other"** as a means of dehumanizing them. **"The other"** is made unworthy of existence. That dehumanization is the spearhead of physical aggression, since the opponent, in this case the Muslims, are considered not only a threat, but also degraded humans. Both Afghanistan and Iraq, as of 2001 and 2003 respectively, have provided the needed foil for atrocities by invading military forces and by the grand opening of Guantanamo which remains open. 9/11 was a calamity inflicted upon the US by a band of maniacs who happened to be born in Muslim lands.

Yet the Trumpists and their clones in other Western States keep on calling **"Islam is not a religion. It is a political ideology."** What a great line for an ISIS on the run to rally its troops especially in West Africa. In this sense, the ultra-right in America and elsewhere have become the ideological stooges of jihadism. To have that horrendous event of 9/11 as a signpost for demonizing 1.7 billion Muslims is a global idiocy. The overwhelming majority of Muslims have condemned that crime. Now the far-flung Muslim world looks upon western reaction to 9/11 as a pretext for persistent cultural and physical aggression against Islam and its adherents. None shall benefit from that myopic vicious cycle except the jihadis. In their present massive retreat in Iraq and Syria, jihadis are in need of that structured anti-Islamism. It is their oxygen tube most needed for survival, even in a splintered status, for their mission of inflicting counter-mischief.

There is little doubt that the era of Trump and Trumpism has ushered in a hurricane of anti-Islamism. The anti-Islamist response to jihadism began in earnest as a structured counter-ideology with the election in 2008 of Barack Obama to the presidency. Being the first Afro-American to reach the Oval Office seems to give the embers of latent racism a new life. Even before the end of the first presidential term of Obama, Donald Trump was at work delegitimizing the President as well as the Office of the presidency. The attacks against Obama were, and continue to be sheer racism barely disguised as anti-Islamism. Obama's middle name **"Hussein"** was a red flag that energized the Trumpist bull.

Obama has delivered a historic speech in 2009 for the Muslim world from Cairo University. It was a message of conciliation and respect for Muslims and their faith. But Donald Trump, a real estate magnate and a wheeler dealer saw an opening to the national scene beyond his TV reality shows. Adopting the conspiracy theory of the extreme right, Trump, as of March 2011 began questioning Obama's religious beliefs and even his right to be president. In a radio interview on March 30, 2011, Trump, without any evidence, said that Obama **"doesn't have a birth certificate. If he does, there's something of that certificate that is very bad for him."**

Then Trump darkly added: **"Now, somebody told me (a regular cover for Trump's fake news) - and I have no idea if this is bad for him or not, but perhaps it would be - that where it (means Obama's birth**

certificate) says 'religion,' it might have Muslim. And if you're a Muslim, you don't change your religion, by the way."[260] The undeniable record shows that Obama is Christian who was born in Hawaii.

But such baseless attacks on Obama's legitimacy as President was Trump's means to gaining prominence in the eyes of the American public as he considered running for president in the 2012 elections. In spite of that smear campaign, Barack Hussein Obama won a second term as President. The process of delegitimation of Obama, a three-dimensional one combining racism, anti-Islamism, and anti-immigration, cannot be divorced from the unintended consequences of providing a **"reason for being"** to jihadism.

The Trump electoral war on Obama, using Islam and public anxiety about America's place in the world, then took on the shape of a movement of exclusivity following June 2015. Announcing his campaign for President that summer, despite his total inexperience in governance, Trump, in late summer of 2015 had to battle 17 other Republicans for the Republican party nomination. His battle cry was **"America First." "America First,"** in the context of Trumpism, was a code name which in its substance could not be distinguishable from the Nazis **"Germany Above All."** (uber alles). The crystallization of white nativism.

That was a winning Trump slogan which secured for him the Republican party nomination for president in the 2016 elections. Subsequently, Trump persevered in his anti-Islam rhetoric with an obvious relish. The public record confirms the hateful claim by Trump that **"I think Islam hates us."** That record includes the following examples:

- His endorsement in New Hampshire in September 2015, nearly two months before winning the Republican party nomination, of a lunatic charge voiced by a man at a campaign town hall meeting. The charge was: **"We have a problem in this country; it's called Muslims. We know our current president (meaning Obama) is one."** This was followed by the same questioner mentioning **"Muslim training camps,"** and asked: **"When can we get rid of them? The response by the would be President of the US, Donald Trump, was: "You know, a lot of people are saying that, and a lot of people are saying that bad things are happening out there. We're going to be looking at that and**

---

[260] Jenna Johnson and Abigail Hauslohner, "A Timeline of Trump's Comments About Islam and Muslims," The Washington Post, May 20, 2017.

plenty of other things."

- Two months later, Trump was asked in November 2015 by a reporter on MSNBC, a cable channel, if he thought **"Islam was an inherently peaceful religion that has been converted by a small percentage of followers or if it is an inherently violent religion."** Trump responded: **"Well, all I can say there is something going on. You know, there's something definitely going on. I don't know that that question can be answered... We are not loved by many Muslims."**

- The Trump campaign did not end in December 2015 before Trump himself, reading aloud to a crowd of supporters in South Carolina what amounted to a declaration of hostility toward Muslims. It reads: **"I Donald J. Trump is calling for a total and complete shutdown of Muslims entering the United States until our country's representatives can figure out what the hell is going on."**

- This was the weaponization of anti-Islamism in the U.S. by a leader running for the presidency of a super power whose Constitution provides for the separation between church and state. The First Amendment of the US Constitution (first of ten amendments ratified on December 15, 1791 as Bill of Rights) begins by: **"Congress shall make no law respecting an establishment of religion, or prohibiting the free exercise thereof."**

- Even before winning the presidency in November 2016, Trump had crossed that constitutional injunction in many ways. On Fox Business in October 2015, he threatened that, if elected, he would **"Certainly look at the idea of closing mosques in the U.S."** A clear denial of the religious rights of more than 7 million American Muslims.

It was within that critical time framework (2014-2016) that ISIS reached its heyday. It established control over large swathes of land in both Syria and Iraq, declared Raqqa, Syria, a seat of the so-called Islamic Caliphate; occupied Mosul, the second largest city in Iraq; and called on all Muslims to join in the war waged by the West on Islam.

Thus, the Trump movement, through declarations made by Trump and the extreme right in America, became a provider for jihadi propaganda whose primary target was to inflict harm on America and the west in general. In 2014, the voices of the new Islamic religious revolution were no match for ideologically responding to either jihadism, or to Trumpist anti-Islamism.

Within a week of becoming President, Trump signed an executive order blocking Syrian refugees and banning citizens of seven Muslim majorities countries from entering the U.S. for 90 days. It was an order which was made to go into effect immediately. It resulted in mass chaos at airports, mass protests, and legal challenges. Calling it a **"Muslim ban,"** he called on Rudolph Giuliani, then a close Trump adviser, to: **"Put a commission together. Show me the right way to do it legally."** It was a case of **"shoot first, think later."**

As if terrorism has a faith, Trump continued to use the term **"radical Islam,"** including in a speech to a joint session of Congress. He had the temerity and the rashness as the American president of attacking a federal judge in Seattle who ruled against his travel ban. The authoritative commentaries included: **"Such challenges to judicial independence cannot be dismissed as mere expressions of pique. They are an important feature of rising authoritarianism."**[261]

In preparation for his first overseas trip as President, which began by a visit to Saudi Arabia, Trump offered a preview of that trip. He declared: **"I'll speak with Muslim leaders (a summit of 50 States) and challenge them to fight hatred and extremism and embrace a peaceful future for their faith… We have to stop radical Islamic terrorism."** Thus Trump, by his own admission, showed his ignorance of the victimization of the Muslim world by terrorism for nearly 20 years, and its attempts by military, police and other means, to extirpate it. Certainly the leaders of the 50 States which attended that summit with Trump had no need for advice on the need to confront jihadism from the promoter of anti-Islamism.

Even the reference to embracing **"a peaceful future for their faith"** reflected Trump's ignorance of what the new Islamic religious revolution, launched since 2014, was all about. It was also an obtuse reference to Islam's **"peaceful future,"** whereas Islam since 1400 years ago has advocated peace.

The ideological origins of that anti-Islamism which stokes the fires of jihadism may lie in the thesis of Harvard's political scientist Samuel Huntington's **"Clash of Civilizations."** The Trumpist anti-Islamic views were but an endorsement of Huntington's warnings about extreme violence with a generalized critique of the Muslim faith. Several of Trump aides like Lt. General Michael Flynn, and Steven Bannon, respectively former Trump's national security adviser and top strategist, have been loyal

---

[261] Noah Feldman and Jacob Weisberg, "What Are Impeachable Offenses?," <u>The New York Review of Books</u>, September 28, 2017, p.20.

adherents to the thesis that the problem of jihadi terrorism had roots in Islam itself, not in the rebellion against Islam called jihadism. This has been their way of **"keeping their base content."**

Such industry of anti-Islamism, promoted at the highest levels of the Trump administration did not proceed unchallenged. **The New York Times** of February 1, 2017 headlined: **"Trump Pushes Dark View of Islam to Center of U.S. Policy-Making."**[262] Pushing back against the ridiculous claim by Trump, the evangelists, and the extreme right wing of the Republican Party, the Times attacked the notion that America was **"under siege by 'radical Islam.'"**

The biggest irony here is that Trump, on his first journey abroad had Saudi Arabia as his first stop. He even performed a sword dance with King Salman and other royals. Was he dancing in Riyadh for business reasons, including billions of dollars worth of American armament? Where was his party's advocacy of America being **"under siege by 'radical Islam'"?**

The New York Times of October 24, 2017 described Riyadh as **"an Oasis for Global Capital."** That was in reference to Saudi Arabia trying to diversify its economy beyond its dependency on oil whose prices are in a free fall. As private jets carrying 3500 business invitees from all over the world were landing in Riyadh, in response to a call from Crown Prince Muhammad Bin Salman, the American Treasury Secretary and a galaxy of Wall Street titans were leading the world's pack who control $22 trillion in assets.

One executive described the gathering as **"a ring-kissing exercise"** in an effort by businesses **"to prove their loyalty… as the country begins to dole out hundreds of billions of dollars as part of its diversification plan known as Vision 2030."** The clear indication of that event which is described as **"Davos In the Desert"** is that the Republican party, which is now splintering unders its new management of Donald Trump and Steve Bannon, has compartmentalized the Muslim world into two: denigration of Islam and elevation of business interests. Unfortunately, the two departments are not so separated by the jihadi propaganda machine.

It was only 10 days after becoming President that Trump told his

---

[262] Scott Shane, Matthew Rosenberg and Eric Lipton, "Trump Pushes Dark View of Islam to Center of U.S. Policy-Making," <u>The New York Times</u>, February 1, 2017.

supporters: **"The hateful ideology of radical Islam must not be allowed to reside or spread within our own communities."**[263] Such anti-Islamism has morphed into public policy championed by Trump in the mistaken belief that attacking the faith of Islam was the way to **"Make America Great Again."**

The series of Trump's executive orders embodying in one form or another Muslim bans were issued against a supportive background of anti-Islamist psychopaths such as General Flynn who had tweeted: **"Fear of Muslims is RATIONAL."** And that **"Islam is not necessarily a religion but a political system that has a religious doctrine behind it."** So it was not enough for the Trumpists to adopt the jihadi interpretation of Islam. It was now the faith itself, and the Governments of the 57 States of the Organization of Islamic Cooperation that were the object of condemnation.

Commenting on the incendiary Trumpist anti-Islamism, Asma Afsaruddin, professor of Islamic studies at Indiana University in the US, said: **"They're tapping into the climate of fear and suspicion since 9/11 ... It's a master narrative that pits the Muslim world against the West ... The executive order(s) will backfire by reinforcing the jihadist line that the United States is at war with Islam ... The White House is a huge soapbox ... The demonization of Muslim and Islam will become even more widespread."**

The ideological enablers of the Trumpist anti-Islamism (in spite of his sword dance with the Saudi monarch), are legion. They include Pamela Geller of **"Stop Islamization of America,"** Robert Spencer of **"Jihad Watch,"** Frank Gaffney, Jr., of **"The Center for Security Policy,"** and Jeff Sessions. Sessions, who had warned of **"the totalitarian threat posed by radical Islam"** is now Attorney General of the U.S., heading the Department of Justice.

It is ironic that while the Grand Imam of Al-Azhar, Dr. Ahmed El-Taiyeb, keeps on advocating anti-Jihadism through the precepts of the new Islamic religious revolution, especially the sanctity of all faiths, the Trumpist movement has emerged as a persistent advocate, for the vilification of Islam. Among the primary megaphones of anti-Islamism is Frank Gaffney, for example. His Center for Security Policy had awarded Jeff Sessions as a Senator its annual **"Keeper of the Flame"** award. The Anti-Defamation League has labelled Gaffney **"the purveyor of anti-Muslim conspiracy**

---

[263] As quoted in <u>The New York Times</u>, <u>Op. Cit.</u>

theories."

The greatest damage to the fabric of friendly relations among nations, codified as an international law principle by the UN Charter of 1945, is the styling and promulgation by the Trump administration of Muslim bans as instruments **"Protecting The Nation From Foreign Terrorist Entry Into the United States"** (January 27, 2017). Section I of that first executive order states, among other things,: **"In order to protect Americans, the United States must ensure that those admitted to this country do not bear hostile attitudes toward it and its founding principles. The United States cannot, and should not, admit those who do not support the Constitution, or those who would place violent ideologies over American law."**[264]

This ban was stopped from taking effect by the federal judiciary, as unconstitutional. But was followed, in a slightly amended form by another ban in the form of an executive order dated March 6, 2017. This subsequent ban designated the nationals of Iran, Libya, Somalia, Sudan, Syria and Yemen as **"nationals (who) continue to present heightened risks to the security of the United States."** Section 1 (e).[265]

A puzzling aspect of these declarations against Muslims and Islam is their being too broad. From a legal perspective, it is too subjective to measure **"attitudes"** in a manner that would not violate the freedom of expression.

When a national security advisor of the President of the United States, namely General Flynn, compares Islam to **"a malignant cancer,"** it follows that Donald Trump should be the focus of this chapter devoted to the phenomenon of **"jihadism being stimulated by anti-Islamism."** Hate begets hate. Anti-Islamism forces jihadism into a role they have long cherished-defenders of Islam from the transgressions of **"the other."** This is happening at the very time that the voice of the new Islamic religious revolution is not reaching American ears. They are voices in Arabic uttered by those who are not savvy in how the modern mind of the West is engaged and influenced.

---

[264] President Trump First Executive Order, understood to be a "Muslim Ban." Issued by the White House on January 27, 2017.

[265] President Trump Second Executive Order, understood to be a "Muslim Ban." Issued by the White House on March 6, 2017.

What lends credibility to the attacks on Islam is largely the terrorist attacks on innocent civilians nearly everywhere. The tiny minority of terrorists, by their criminal actions, provides the anti-Islamists with what they seek: validating their warring on Islam itself. This equation is made more complex by other extraneous factors. Chief among these are the brutal civil wars raging in Syria and Yemen; the ethos of Wahhabism where women in Saudi Arabia are finally permitted to drive cars (modest progress for gender equality), and the non-conformity of the millions of refugees, mostly Muslims, with the laws of the host countries, mostly non-Muslim.

The rise of nativism, the decline of the concept of globalism, and the fear-mongering engaged in by those who call for stopping the so-called **"Islamization of Europe"** are real factors in the dangerous tilt toward anti-Islamism.

The battle of justice for Islam and Muslims has undoubtedly been helped, not only by the American judiciary which has been attacked by Trump as biased. But also by universities, liberal media, and many human rights organizations including even those which have been mistakenly charitable towards the Muslim Brotherhood (a terrorist incubator).

A prime example of American academic support for the constitutional rights of American Muslims under the concept of separation of church from state is the Brennan Center for Justice of the New York University School of Law. In its report of April 19, 2017, it cites **"at least five forms ... tangibly harming the American Muslim community: the use of anti-Muslim rhetoric; the elevation of Islamophobic staff members to key positions in the White House; the ban on visitors from seven Muslim-majority countries from entering the country; the goal of making vetting procedures 'extreme' for potential visitors and immigrants; and a lack of response to the rise in hate crimes targeted at Muslims and other groups."[266]**

In the process of the gathering by the US Department of Homeland Security of social media on people, naturalized citizens have been included. This matter has now matured into a case to be argued in 2017 before the Supreme Court of the U.S., whose majority of 5 to 9 justices are now

---

[266] Faiza Patel, Rachel Levinson-Waldman, "The Islamophobic Administration," <u>Brennan Center for Justice at the New York University School of Law</u>, April 19, 2017.

considered conservative, expected to side with the Executive branch.[267]

Nothing could reflect the division within American society of today more than the march by white nationalists on the University of Virginia campus in August 2017. This saga continues to play out on the world stage in the form of an America isolating itself from the rest of the world.

It is unprecedented for an American Secretary of State to call his president names. But Rex Tillerson called President Trump **"a moron."** It is also unprecedented for a senior Republican Senator to attack the character and fitness for office of his president who is also a Republican. But Senator Bob Corker of Tennessee who heads the Senate Foreign Relations Committee called Trump worse than that. In an interview with the **New York Times,** Corker said that Trump was treating his office like **"a reality show, with reckless threats toward other countries that set the nation on the path to World War III… He concerns me. He would have to concern anyone who cares about our nation."**[268]

This may possibly signal a premature end of the Trump presidency. It seems that Donald Trump who, at the UN in September 2017, threatened to wipe North Korea off the map, has become a concern for the entire world. As to the reaction by the Republican Congressional leadership, no one rose up to counter Senator Corker's assessment of Trump as a danger to his nation. On the contrary. Comments by that leadership have been to praise the integrity of that outspoken member of that leadership.

Complex issues, like these presented in this volume, have no definitive answers. The reason does not lie only in their complexity. For that complexity is further made more confusing because the structure and contents of these issues remain in constant flux. Jihadism is the rebirth of a new type of globalized war. Camouflaging is religious, mixing revived nationalisms with a cultural anti-Islamic fervor, all ignited by various actors with conflicting agendas and ideologies.

To cite some of the main symptoms, we refer without elaboration to the following phenomena: While Wahhabism seems to be receding in Saudi

---

[267] Timothy Ivory Carpenter v. United States of America, A Case Before the U.S. Supreme Court for arguments in 2017. (Re the Privacy Act of 1974; System of Records).

[268] The New York Times, October 9, 2017, p. A1.

Arabia, Ottomanism is reasserting itself in Turkey. In Netherlands, one of the most progressive European countries, defeat of the extreme right has resulted in a Dutch governing coalition moving even further to the right - the incubator of anti-Islamism. In Myanmar, whose president Aung San Suu Kyi is a Nobel Peace laureate, has defended its country's ethnic cleansing of Rohingyas.

More of this confusing panorama: The Syrian civil war of 7 years shows no sign of abatement. And chemical warfare has been waged by an Assad regime seeking, hopelessly, to rule over a united Syria. A non-veiled young woman, Maryam Nawaz Sharif, might become the second female prime minister of Pakistan. Yet for stupid religious reasons, the Shiis are being persecuted in that country. And the jihadis, while losing territory as cohesive organizations, are splintering throughout territories now regarded as no man's land.

In spite of all these conflicting cross-currents, the weapon of ideology in warring on jihadism remains, though presently under-used, a viable instrument of confrontation of that evil. As UNESCO proclaims and we paraphrase: **"war begins in peoples' mind."** Hence the mind should be our arena of determined struggle.

ANNEX I

Omar's Instructions

Issued in the Arabic of Quraish By Omar Ibn Al-Khattab The Second Caliph after the Prophet Muhammad. To a nominee for a judgeship in Kofa, Iraq. (Omar, the first to be called Prince of the Faithful, ruled from 634 to 644 AD. Was known for his sense of absolute justice)

- From Omar To Abu-Musa Al-Ashaari: Peace Be Upon You!!
- Know that judging is a firm religious duty, and a tradition observed. Be sure to understand the pleadings delivered before you. And when you reach a decision based on evidence, implement it. For there is no use in speaking about what is right if it lacks execution.
- Maintain a neutral face while on the bench, performing the role of a judge. This way ensures that the powerful shall not aspire to your siding unjustly with them. Nor shall the powerless despair of your rendering justice unto them.
- The burden of proof is upon the plaintiff. And those impeaching that evidence should take a solemn oath that their denial has merit.
- Conciliation is permissible between litigants (referred to in general as Muslims). That is unless it is on a basis disapproved by Islamic jurisprudence, or denying what is permitted under that jurisprudence.
- Do not hesitate to review and amend a judgment which you might have reached the day before, only to discover, through your sense of fairness, that it was in error. That is because what is right does not age by the passage of time, as nothing could invalidate an obvious right.
- Returning to the zone of what is rightfully just supersedes any

continuation down the path of what is unjust. And if someone claims a right that has not been uncovered before a proof was available, give them a time limit to provide such evidence. If they succeed, rule in favor of restituting to them those rights. But if they fail, they lose their cause. Thus no pretexts can stand, and no blindness to what is evident can prevail.

- Comprehension, comprehension of the pleadings in your court, especially whatever is in those pleadings not based on text either in the Quran or in the Prophet's tradition. In these situations, resort to prior cases decided by unanimity (ijmaa) or by analogy (quias). Educate yourself about those precedents, then make the judgments which seem to you to be supported by the Quran, as close as possible to the word of God, and nearest to the concept of fairness.

- People (the faithful) have a sense of what is right within their society. With the exception of those whose testimony had been previously impeached as false, and of those previously convicted, and of those whose sense of loyalty or family lineage is subject to doubt.

- Only God knows what people harbor in their bosoms and He is the One who shields them from punitive measures. That is with the exception of situations where there is probative evidence and proven faith.

- You are hereby instructed to avoid becoming angry or anxious or bored, or upset by adversaries, or turning your back upon issues of conflict. That is because good judging on issues of right and wrong is what God dictates to you and is what you shall be remembered by.

- This is applicable to judges who are endowed with good will and who might rule even against themselves. It is the way prescribed by God for any relationship between a judge and his community.

- But those who resort to mere appearances which they know to be non-reflective of their true feelings, shall not be favored by God. Only honesty can be favored by God, and that is where God shall favor those who adhere to it, rewarding them in their livelihoods and through his limitless mercy.

Peace Be With You.

بسم الله الرحمن الرحيم

رسالة عمر بن الخطاب

إلى أبي موسى الأشعري عندما وَلّاه قضاء الكوفه

"من عبد الله عمر أمير المؤمنين

إلى عبد الله بن قيس"

سلام عليك ...

أما بعد – فإن القضاء فريضةٌ محكمة وسنَّة متَّبعة فافهم إذا أُدلي إليك وانفذ إذا تبين لك فإنه لا ينفع تكلُّم بحق لا نفاذ له.

آس بين الناس في مجلسك وفي وجهك وقضائك حتى لا يطمع شريف في حيفك ولا يأس ضعيف من عدلك.

البيّنة على مَن ادّعى واليمين على مَن أنكر، والصلح جائز بين المسلمين إلا صُلحًا أحلَّ حرامًا أو حرَّم حلالًا ولا يمنعك قضاءٌ قضيته بالأمس فراجعت فيه نفسك وهديت فيه لرشدك أن تُراجع فيه الحق فإن الحق قديمٌ لا يبطله شيء.

والرجوع إلى الحق خير من التمادي في الباطل ومن ادعى حقا غائبا أو بيّنة فاضرب له أمدا ينتهي إليه، فإن بيّنه أعطيته بحقه وإن أعجزه ذلك استحللت عليه القضية، فإن ذلك أبلغ للعذر "وأجلى للعمى".

الفهم ... الفهم فيما أُدلي إليك مما ورد عليك مما ليس في قرآن ولا سُنَّة ثم قايس الأمور عندئذ واعرف الأمثال ثم أعمد فيما ترى إلى أقربها إلى الله وأشبَهها بالحق. المسلمون عدول بعضهم على بعض إلا مجرّبًا عليه شهادة زور أو مجلودًا في حدٍّ أو ظنينًا في ولاء أو قرابة، فإن الله تولى من عباده السرائر وستر عليهم الحدود إلا بالبيّنات والإيمان.

وإياك والغضب والقلق والضجر والتأذي بالخصوم والتنكُّر عند الخصومات فإن القضاء في مواطن الحق مما يوجب الله به الأجر ويحسن به الذكر فمن خلُصت نيته في الحق ولو على نفسه كفاه الله ما بينه وبين الناس ومن تزيَّن بما ليس في نفسه شأنه فإن الله تعالى لا يقبل من العباد إلا ما كان خالصًا فما ظنك بثواب عند الله في عاجل رزقه وخزائن رحمته.

"والسلام عليكم ورحمة الله"

ANNEX II

Brief Note on Al-Azhar Al-Shareef (Al-Sharif)

Built as a mosque in Cairo in 972 AD by Jawhar Al-Siqqilli (the Sicilian) and has been, throughout its history, the iconic citadel for Islamic learning. In 1936, Al-Azhar became also a university consisting of various colleges. Its curriculum was originally focused upon the Arabic language and Sharia (Islamic law). Later the curriculum expanded to include various fields of modern knowledge. Its present Grand Imam is Dr. Ahmed El-Taiyeb (see his short bio in these annexes).

It is with pride that I should note that one of Al-Azhar graduates was my late father, Sheikh El-Sayed Muhammad Hassanain El-Ayouty, from whom I have inherited the great affection for Al-Azhar which is now leading the New Islamic Religious Revolution.

In its Article 7, the Egyptian Constitution of 2014 has provided that: **"Al-Azhar Al-Shareef is an independent Islamic institution devoted to the diffusion of knowledge. It handles all its affairs on its own, and is the principal point of reference (Marjiyyah) in religious and Islamic matters. It is also tasked with the responsibility for advocacy for faith, and for the instruction about religion and the Arabic language in Egypt and abroad. The State provides the necessary budget provisions enabling Al-Azhar to carry out its tasks.**

The Imam of Al-Azhar is independent, and cannot be removed from office. Relevant law provides for the method by which he is appointed and his selection shall be from among the Group of Grand Scholars."

Throughout its history, Al-Azhar, especially as of the 19th century, has also been the incubator of the Egyptian and other national struggles for the right to self-determination and independence. Its role in these liberation causes, particularly as of Napoleon's invasion of Egypt in 1898, is celebrated in the annals of Egyptian history.

At present, following the 2014 call by President Abdel-Fattah El-Sisi and the spectrum of the secular leadership of Egypt for a new Islamic religious revolution countering jihadism, Al-Azhar has assumed its rightful place in leading that ideological counter-attack against terrorism.

ANNEX III

The Grand Imam of Al-Azhar Al-Sharif
Dr. Ahmed Muhammad El-Taiyeb
A Biographical Note

Raised in a house of learning in Luxor province, Egypt, the Grand Imam of Al-Azhar joined that iconic institution where he memorized the Quran and delved into the corpus of Islamic scholarship. Graduating in 1969 with a B.A. with distinction from the Department of Creed and Philosophy, he went on to earn from the same department at Al-Azhar University an M.A. (1971) and a Ph.D. (1977).

Dr. El-Taiyeb was appointed the Grand Mufti of Egypt in 2002 by presidential decree, and in 2003 he was appointed President of Al-Azhar University. In 2010, he was appointed the Grand Imam of Al-Azhar, succeeding the late Grand Imam Muhammad Tantawi.

He founded the World Association of Al-Azhar Graduates (WAAG) and worked for other Islamic universities in Saudi Arabia, Qatar, the United Arab Emirates and Pakistan.

An active participant in many Islamic and international conferences, he has, over the years, attended such events including in France, Indonesia, Italy, Jordan (The Royal Aal Al-Bayt Institute for Islamic Thought), Switzerland, and the United States. His membership in societies in Egypt covers the Supreme Council for Islamic Affairs, the Islamic Research Academy, the Egyptian Philosophical Society, the Board of Trustees of the Radio and TV Union, and the Ministry of Education Committee on educational standards. He is also the recipient of several international awards and honors.

Dr. El-Taiyeb has kept his academic experiences and contributions, including his extended stint at the University of Paris, renewable. His written works have largely centered on Islamic philosophy, logic, and comparative thought. He has translated several works from French into Arabic, and has presented several papers on **"The Necessities of Renewal"** at symposia held in both Europe and Egypt.

ANNEX IV

Al-Azhar Document on Egypt's Future

On August 17, 2011 Al-Azhar Al-Sharif issued this document enunciated by the Grand Imam of Al-Azhar, Dr. Ahmed El-Taiyeb,billed: **"Al-Azhar Document on Egypt's Future."** It is the product of a unique consensus among leaders of various fields of faith, politics, law, art, literature, history, society,   psychology,   and   other   areas   of   academe.

Out of the turbulence of the Revolution of January 25, 211 which swept aside the military rule of 60 years, emerged this consensual document of guidelines for constitutional formulation. All aspirants to the presidency of Egypt, all leaders of all parties and of various fields of thought, all opinion-makers of various stripes, including the Coptic community, sat at the Grand Imam's   rectangular   table   to   say,   "yes"   to   those   guidelines.

Al-Azhar document whose text was made public at a press conference at Al-Azhar on August 17, 2011, took into account those inimitable Egyptian perspectives anchored in Islamic jurisprudence; Al-Azhar's history of struggle for freedom and independence; the civilizational depth which merges physical sciences with social sciences and the arts; the political perspectives whereby future decision -makers of Egypt are nurtured; and the linkage between knowledge, renaissance, and cultural resurgence in the Arab   homeland   and   the   Islamic   world.

The names of great lights of Al-Azhar, especially in the modern era, were cited bringing them back from beyond the grave to historic prominence, such as: Sheikh Al-Islam Hassan El-Attar; his disciple Sheikh Rifaa El-Tahtawi; Sheikh Muhammad Abdo, the great modern reformer; Sheikh Al-Maraghy, together with other Al-Azhar leaders of reform such as

Muhammad Abdullah Diraz, Mustapha Abdel-Razik, and last but not least, the venerable Sheikh Shaltout, and the late Sheikh Muhammad Tantawi.

The Al-Azhar document frames the following principles which have guided the drafters of Egypt's 2014 secular Constitution within eleven such principles. These, in summary, are:

- **First:** Egypt as a State is based upon a constitutional democracy with separation of powers, of which the legislative power is to be exercised by the people's representatives. Islam, in its legislation, civilization, and history does not recognize a "religiously-based" State. The overall arching principles of Islamic law (Sharia) are the primary source of legislation, providing that the adherents of other religions are guaranteed, in their personal status cases, resort to their own religious laws.
- **Second:** Democratic rule is based on free and direct elections, which encapsulate the modern formulation of the application of the Islamic precepts of Shura (consultation). Such rule guarantees diversity, the peaceful transfer of power, a well-defined exercise of authority whose custodians are accountable to the people's representatives with a view to the provision of public service, subject only to the rule of law. Corruption is punishable under the law, and transparency and the freedom and transmission of information are to be applied.
- **Third:** Commitment to basic rights and freedoms with regard to both thought and opinion, including full respect of the rights of the individual, of women and children, and of the principle of diversity. Citizenship is the primary basis from which emanates obligations to society.
- **Fourth:** Full respect to the view of the other, which implicates the necessity of avoidance of declaring others to be apostates, traitors, or the abuse of religion for the purposes of sowing divisiveness and hatred among the citizens. Sectarian conflict and racist advocacy are criminally injurious to the homeland.
- **Fifth:** Commitment to international covenants (treaties) and decisions (declarations), and to civilizational norms and accomplishments in human (friendly) relationships which accord with the Islamic and Arab traditions of tolerance and with the long experience of the Egyptian people throughout its historical periods which produced luminous examples of peaceful co-existence and the striving towards humanity's benefits as a whole.
- **Sixth:** Full attention to the dignity of the Egyptian nation and its national pride, and to an assured protection of places of worship of

all faiths, and of the freedom of expression and artistic and literary expression.

- **Seventh:** Education, scientific research, and the embarking upon the age of knowledge (information) are to be regarded the locomotive of Egypt's civilizational progress, including the eradication of illiteracy.
- **Eighth:** Implementation of the ladder (jurisprudence) of priorities with regard to the achievement of development, social justice, confrontation of oppression (hegemony) and of corruption, elimination of unemployment, all within the recognition of veritable and serious health care as a duty of the State towards all citizens.
- **Ninth:** The establishment of Egypt's solid relationships with its sister Arab States, as well as States within its Islamic, African and other international spheres, along with support of Palestinian rights, of safe-guarding the independence of Egypt's decision-making (will), and of the re-establishment of Egypt's traditional and historical leadership role as the basis of cooperation for the universal good, and of environmental protection and just peace among nations.
- **Tenth:** Enhancement of the independence of the instituitoin of Al-Azhar, and the resurrection of the "Commission of Grand Ulamas (Islamic Scholars)" endowed with responsibility for the appointment through elections of the Rector of Al-Azhar.
- **Eleventh:** Recognition of Al-Azhar "Al-Sharif" as the source and focus of responsibility to which reference should be made in all matters of Islam, its disciplines, its traditions, and its jurisdictional interpretation (ijtihad) and modern thought patterns. This is without the elimination of the right of all to the voicing of opinions on the basis of recognizable and acceptable scientific parameters.

ANNEX V

On Martyring Clergyman Shehatah

The tragedy is beyond condolences. Especially that it is a part of a destructive pattern which overtook our shared Egypt as of 1952. Prayers are in order. But prayers must be accompanied by action: Application of justice to the fullest to the assassin, and a thought campaign for anti-Jihadi cleansing. I, for one, an Egyptian born in an Azhari home in the province of Sharqiah, shall do my part. Thus the following is not a self-serving commercial for which I have no need. I have finished authoring a new book in English, titled **"War On Jihadism By Ideology: The New Islamic Religious Revolution."** It shall be published by Amazon in 2017. Its Foreword ends with a lament for our martyred Brother - in - Faith Samaan Shehatah. His assailant needs to be made a public example of The New Egypt. It is the Egypt of post - The Muslim Brotherhood whose remnants is Salafism -- The Theocracy which was never supported by Islamic jurisprudence. For Islam did not create a State. It created a Community. And when a so-called **"sheikh"** proclaims that the assassin of Al-Qummos Shehtah should be spared capital punishment (A Muslim Killing A Kafir -- as he argued), that person should be charged with Daesh advocacy. The cloud over Egypt is dissipating. Let us all resolve to honor the Shehatah martyrdom by hastening the remergence of the SUN of Ikhnaton, the Father of Monotheism --The One-ness of our Creator. The preamble of the the 2014 Egyptian Constitution proclaims in its para. 7: **"On Egypt's soil, the Egyptians welcomed to their bossom Our Lady, The Virgin Mary, and her Baby, then offered thousands of martyrs in defending the Church of our lord Jesus, may peace be upon him."**

ANNEX VI

Jihadism As Global Warfare - The Egyptian Front

PROLOGUE: From Cairo to New York City, From Ottawa to Nice. And from Abuja to Mosul. Jihadism, though diminished, is still fighting. Felling the innocent and the defender, whether a clergyman, a cyclist, a soldier, or a female child held as a human shield by inhuman hands. Under the guise of Islam, using **"God Is Great"** as a prelude to butchery. Against this background on a sputtering jihadi warfare, SUNSGLOW, through this panel, examines various aspects of this globalized warfare, including a salute to all martyrs, taking the Egyptian front as a case study.

Date: Thursday, November 6, 2017 (6:00 pm - 8:00 pm)
Place: The Thurgood Marshall US Courthouse, 40 Foley Square, Manhattan
Hosted By: The Honorable District Court Judge, Paul G. Gardephe. Jury Room 705.
Panel of 6   (in the order of speaking for 15 minutes each in English)
  (1) H.E. Ambassador Dr. Hesham Elnakib, Consul General of Egypt in New York (on Egypt's Confrontation of Jihadism)
  (2) Father Gregory Saroufeem, Coptic Priest (on the concept of martyrdom)
  (3) Father Brian Jordan, OFM, Chaplain, St. Franci College, Brooklyn, New York (on the power of love as faith)
  (4) Mr. Moheb Ghabour, Editor-in-Chief of Voice of Belady (in Arabic, with consecutive translation in English, on Coptic/Muslim unity)
  (5) The Honorable District Court Judge Paul G. Gardephe (on prosecuting hate crimes under American laws)
  (6) Dr. Yassin El-Ayouty, Esq. (on the one-ness of God {Tawheed}

under Islamic Law)

ANNEX VII

Nizar Qabbani: A Syrian Poet: Imagining a Dictator's Soliloquy About His Indispensability

Soliloquy of a Dictator: **"Whenever I thought of relinquishing power?!"** It is a poem by the famous Syrian poet and songwriter, Nizar Qabbani. The original is in Arabic, translated into English by this author. It is intended to focus on the magic of folklore in the Arab Spring, and on why people revolt.

Now to the Nizar Qabbani poem:

WHENEVER I THOUGHT OF RELINQUISHING POWER!

Whenever I thought of relinquishing power
My conscience stood in the way

After I am gone
who will rule these good people?

After me
who will cure the limp
the leper
the blind?
who will raise the dead?

And from whose overcoat
will the light of the moon shine?

And who will bestow on

the people the gift of rain?

And who will whip them
ninety lashings?

And who will hang them
from the limbs of trees?

And who will force them
to live like herds of cows?
And perish as cows perish?

Whenever I think of
relinquishing power?

My eyes fill out with tears
as if they were a rain cloud.

So let my fate to rule stand, for it is
my destiny

And it shall be from now until
the end of time.

ANNEX VIII

List of My Authored and Co-Authored Books

Not including articles, expert reports, field studies, and lectures, the book titles are:
   (1) Refugees South of the Sahara: An African Dilemma (New York: Nego Universities Press, 1970);
   (2) The UN and Decolonization: The Role of Afro-Asia (The Hague: Nijhoff, 1971);
   (3) Africa and International Organization (The Hague: Nijhoff, 1974);
   (4) The Organization of African Unity (The OAU) After Ten Years (New York: Praeger, 1975 and 1976);
   (5) The OAU After Twenty Years (New York: Praeger, 1984);
   (6) The OAU After Thirty Years (Westport, Conn.: Praeger, 1994);
   (7) Government Ethics and Law Enforcement (Westport, Conn.: Praeger, 2000);
   (8) Perspectives on 9/11 (Westport, Conn.: Heinemann/Praeger, 2004);
   (9) The Transformation of Egypt Through Revolution: 2011-2014 (New York, Amazon, 2015);
   (10) The New Egypt: From Chaos to the Strong State: 2014-2016 (New York: Amazon/Createspace/Kindle, 2016).

In Arabic:
   (1) America's Imperial Security (Cairo: The Egyptian Council for Foreign Affairs, 2007);
   (2) An Impostor in the Village {Dajjal Fi Qariah} (Cairo: Aalam Al-Kotob, 2013). On the abuse of beliefs for sordid ends. First published in Cairo in 1948.
   (3) Forthcoming: Between Sunnis and Shiis: No Cleavage Except on

Imam Ali's Succession
(4) Forthcoming: Saad Zaghloul - Father of Egypt's Independence.

Blog - Postings at: http://tahrirforever.blogspot.com

ABOUT THE AUTHOR

Dr. Yassin El-Ayouty, Esq. is an attorney and professor of law and politics, residing in New York. He has a has a Ph.D. from New York University in international law and international organization(1966); and J.D. from Cardozo School of Law (1994). A U.S. Fulbright Scholar (1952-1954); recipient of N.Y.U. Founders Day Award, and Cardozo Faculty Award for Best Legal Writing. University professor since 1966; and Distinguished Visiting Professor, Nova Law Center, Fort Lauderdale, Florida. Member of American bars and Federation of Arab Bars. Practising litigation in America and abroad. Served the UN for 32 years, retiring as Political Director. Co-founded UNITAR; drafted its Statute for UN General Assembly (1965). UN Representative of the Egyptian Council for Foreign Affairs (Cairo); Established SUNSGLOW-Global Training in the Rule of Law in 1998, now a nonprofit with a center in Toronto. Presently, Professor at Fordham University School of Law, teaching "Islamic Law and Global Security;" St. Francis College (New York City); Cairo University Law; Focal point in North America for Al-Azhar University (Cairo); and Emeritus Professor at Stony Brook University, New York. Research and blogging focus: Islamic Law; the New Egypt; US/Arab strategic relations. Blogger and author in English and Arabic of articles and books, the most recent of which, preceding the present volume is "The New Egypt: From Chaos To The Strong State"(Amazon, 2016).

www.ingramcontent.com/pod-product-compliance
Lightning Source LLC
Chambersburg PA
CBHW050910260726
48660CB00001B/127